vastu

vastu

Ashwinie Kumar Bansal

BARRON'S

A QUARTO BOOK

All inquiries should be addressed to:
Barron's Educational Series, Inc.
250 Wireless Boulevard
Hauppauge, NY 11788
http://www.barronseduc.com

International Standard Book Number 0-7641-2106-5

Library of Congress Catalog Card Number
2001092588

QUAR.SHAS

Conceived, designed and produced by
Quarto Publishing plc
The Old Brewery
6 Blundell Street
London N7 9BH

Senior project editor   Nicolette Linton
Art editor   Jill Mumford
Assistant art director   Penny Cobb
Text editor   Sally MacEachern
Designer   Jill Mumford
Illustrator Mark Duffin and Martin Saunders
Photographer   Colin Bowling
Picture research   Sandra Assersohn
Proofreader   Pat Farrington
Indexer   Pamela Ellis

Art director   Moira Clinch
Publisher   Piers Spence

Manufactured by Universal Graphics Pte Ltd, Singapore
Printed by Leefung-Asco Printers Ltd, China

9 8 7 6 5 4 3 2 1

AUTHOR'S ACKNOWLEDGMENTS
Thanks go to Mrs. Pramjit Kaur Bhutani, Mr. Devender Singh
Rawat, and Mr. Bagat Singh Bist for their assistance, and to
everyone else involved in producing this book.

CONTENTS

The wise man looks into space and does not regard the small as too little
nor the great as too big; for he knows that there is no limit to dimensions.
Lao Tzu

introduction *to vastu*

Vastu, the ancient Hindu science of design and architecture, has its roots in Vedic philosophy (the four-volume Vedas are also the foundation of Hinduism, yoga, and ayurveda). Vastu is widely practiced in India but has only recently spread to the West. Some practitioners maintain that, centuries ago, Buddhist monks and other travelers took the principles of Vastu to China; adapted to local conditions, it became known as feng shui.

VASTU SHASTRAS

Vastu-inspired architecture, iconography, and methods of construction have been passed down through generations and are laid out in ancient texts called *Vastu Shastras*, said to have been written in the sixth century A.D to provide guidelines for the design and construction of towns, palaces, temples, and homes. A section of the *shastras*, known as the *Vastu Vidya*, deals specifically with architectural rules, that some believe were based on laws written by Vishwakarma, the celestial architect. The *shastras* offer detailed guidelines to selecting a lucky site for a building. The correct placement and orientation of the building is vital in Vastu, and special rituals were observed to chase spirits from a site and to bless the gods.

Vastu is a mixture of spiritual philosophy and science. Although its language is couched in that of myth and its precepts in the form of stories about the gods, the advice it gives is both practical and wise. You will bring balance and harmony into your home and your life by following these eternal principles.

LIVING WITH VASTU *(left)*
Although originally used as an aid to planning and building Indian homes, the most basic advice that Vastu Shastra *gives—to create homes in line with the laws of nature and the cosmos—makes an environmentally friendly, harmonious home, whether you live in the northern or southern hemisphere.*

THE RULES OF NATURE

Vastu is not just about design, form, utility, and durability—the concepts that usually define architecture. It enables us to align our plots and houses in accordance with the rules of nature to make the best use of interior space, and to arrange the contents of our homes so that they create order and balance, resulting in a harmonious and relaxing atmosphere, which promotes our well-being and happiness.

Vastu is the oldest nature-friendly form of construction. This ancient science of architecture helps us create user-friendly designs that are closely connected to nature and the cosmic energies in the environment. Vastu lays great stress on knowing and honoring the deities associated with the cardinal directions and their related elements. By following the natural order of the universe, we can learn to incorporate harmony into constructed spaces. When a home is soothing and tranquil, it helps the mind attain peace, a state essential for good health.

Vastu teaches that we humans should maintain in our lives the balance and systematic orderliness that is so evident in the universe. The cosmos follows a pattern laid down since time immemorial. For instance, a key principle of Vastu is that the center of both a home and a room should be kept open and clear of clutter. When we leave the center space open we honor Lord Brahma, the creator of the universe, whose realm is the *brahmasthana* (central space). Positive energy concentrates in the *brahmasthana* and radiates from there to all the other directions of the house. In practical terms an uncluttered central area makes a room look open and spacious.

APPLYING VASTU

An experienced Vastu practitioner or *vastushastri* will examine the interior of a building with the intention of fortifying and strengthening the five elements —fire, water, earth, air, and space. When the elements are balanced they direct positive cosmic energy into the home, bringing peace to the minds of the inhabitants and joy to their hearts.

Hindus believe that, if the principles of Vastu are incorporated into a home, peace reigns within it. As a result the inhabitants'

VISHWAKARMA
(left)

Vishwakarma, the architect of the gods, is usually depicted holding tools and a book.

concentration improves, enabling them to make the right decisions about family, work, and business. In an office tensions and stress are removed; people work more effectively, resulting in success and financial gain for the company.

Vastu puts people in harmony with their home and their home in harmony with the universe by applying rules concerning the five elements and the cardinal directions. Following its principles will enable you to create a holistic space that will make you at one with your environment, rather than at odds with it.

FIRST IMPRESSIONS *(above)*

The main entrance represents the mouth of the dæmon Vastu Purusha and should always be larger and more decorative than the other doors in the house. Green is an auspicious color for doors.

A HAPPY HOME *(above)*

Follow Vastu guidelines when planning your home (as shown on pages 48–51 and 66–69), and you can bring harmony and well-being to your family.

HOW TO USE THIS BOOK

This book is invaluable when making any decisions connected with the home. It offers advice about choosing a new home or adapting an existing house, and on decorating the interior in line with Vastu principles.

If you plan to make major structural changes to a house, you should consult an experienced *vastushastri* before making any decisions. A Vastu expert may be able to suggest remedial measures that do not involve construction work, saving you unnecessary expense. In addition, it is advisable to consult an architect or builder. You do not have to spend a lot of money to apply the Vastu principles described in this book. Its aim is to bring peace, harmony, success, and prosperity into your life.

PHOTO OF ELEMENT

QUALITIES OF ELEMENT

COLOR-CODED CORNERS

DEITY ASSOCIATED WITH ELEMENT

ROOM PLAN

FEEDBACK ON FLOOR PLANS GIVING VASTU ADVICE

ROOM ASSOCIATED WITH DIRECTION

COMPASS SHOWING DIRECTION

COLOR-CODED CORNERS

COLORS OF ROOMS ACCORDING TO THE VASTU MANDALA

COLOR-CODED CORNERS

EXAMPLES OF COLOR COMBINATIONS

ILLUSTRATIONS EXPLAINING COLOR THEORY

the *history and philosophy of vastu*

With its roots in ancient Vedic culture, Vastu philosophy teaches that our physical and spiritual well-being depends on our harmonious relationship with the space that surrounds us. Vastu is considered by many Hindus to be an architectural science and its construction blueprint—the Vastu Purusha Mandala—has been instrumental in the planning, building, and decorating of Indian homes and buildings for many centuries.

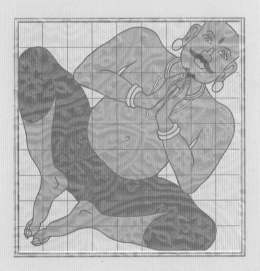

O god of structures and buildings, we are your devotees.
Listen to our prayers, keep us free of disease, give us wealth and prosperity,
and look after the wellbeing of all people and animals living in this house.

Prayer to Vastu Purusha, *Rig-Veda*

vastu purusha *mandala*

The Vastu Purusha Mandala—the square grid at the center of the philosophy and science of Vastu—is a representation of the Hindu view of the universe. Vastu practitioners and architects use it as a blueprint for constructing buildings and designing interiors that are spiritually uplifting and harmonious. Within the mandala lies the figure of the legendary dæmon, Vastu Purusha, pinned down by 45 deities on the instruction of Lord Brahma. Vastu Purusha is symbolic of the harmful energy that can exist in a building site if the spirits of the site are not appeased and the gods blessed. He can bring prosperity and happiness to those who build and design their homes in line with ancient Vastu principles.

VASTU PURUSHA MANDALA

(right and above)

The dæmon Vastu Purusha lies facedown in the square mandala, facing the ground, with his body aligned along the northeast/southwest axis. Each square within the mandala corresponds to a part of the body, and certain points —the marma sthanas—are vulnerable to heavy objects being placed over them.

TAMING THE DÆMON

According to Indian mythology, the legendary Vastu Purusha was a brutal dæmon who harassed humans and gods alike, and caused massive destruction in the world. The gods grouped together to fight back. They went to Lord Brahma for help, begging him to capture the dæmon. Lord Brahma fought and beat the Vastu Purusha, and ordered the 45 gods to pin him to the ground in the position where he now lies in the mandala.

The dæmon appealed to Lord Brahma's mercy, and eventually Brahma declared that Vastu Purusha would gain fame and immortality as the Lord of Construction. The creator of the universe insisted that the dæmon was to ensure the happiness of those people who offered him prayers and solicited his blessings before initiating the construction of a building.

Lord Brahma said that all buildings should be oriented and constructed in such a manner that they kept both the presiding deities (who remained in position and became associated with particular directions) and the Vastu Purusha happy, comfortable, and contented.

MARMA STHANAS

Marma sthanas are the most sensitive points on Vastu Purusha's body, such as the heart, chest, and navel. These points cluster in the center of the building, called the *Brahmasthana*. Heavy structures like pillars, beams, walls, doors, and closets should not be built or positioned over these points. Shifting heavy structures to the right or left of the points can be a good compromise.

THE MANDALA

The mandala—when used as a construction blueprint rather than a meditational tool—is a design within a square. The square is associated with the masculine principle, Purusha, and the building is the feminine principle. The grid is divided into 1, 4, 9, 16, 25, 36, 49, 64,

LORD BRAHMA

(left)

In Hindu mythology, the creator of the universe fought and overcame the dæmon Vastu Purusha, with the help of 45 deities. Lord Brahma —along with Lord Shiva and Lord Vishnu—make up the Hindu trinity.

81, 100, or more squares, in an arithmetic progression, resulting in 32 different mandalas with 1,024 squares and further subdivisions. To read the squares, follow a circular path from the center to the edge of the mandala. The 45 deities are placed systematically within the squares and their subdivisions.

THE GODS AND THE RISHIS

Each square in the mandala is named for a god. When designing a home, it is important to apply Vastu principles in such a way that the gods are honored. In India offerings are made to the gods before construction begins, as each square is completed, and when the house is finished. So, for example, offerings will be made to Vishwakarma, the architect of the gods, and Lord Brahma, the creator of the universe, at the center of the home —the heart of Vastu Purusha.

The ancient *rishis*, who first allotted specific deities to the plan of the mandala, had a vast knowledge of the cosmic energies of the universe. These wise men were aware of the effects of sunlight, and the colors of the spectrum. They accepted the gifts and detriments of solar energy; and they observed that, as the sun moves from the east to the west, its rays undergo certain changes. Accordingly, the ancient architects planned homes where the rooms received the beneficial rays of the sun at all times.

LORD VISHNU *(left)*

Vishnu, the preserver of the universe, is a merciful god. His four hands hold sacred objects: a lotus flower, a conch shell, a chakra (wheel), and a mace.

VASTU PURUSHA AND THE HOME

The head of the Vastu Purusha is in the northeast direction; this area of the building should be kept open and cool with water features, such as ponds or fountains.

The arms of the dæmon are to the left and right of the head, facing north and east. These areas should be kept as open as possible, to make the Vastu Purusha more comfortable. Also, make sure to avoid weighty constructions in this area.

The Vastu Purusha's thighs are in the south and west corners of the mandala. Storage areas, closets, and stairs should be placed in these parts of the building because the thighs are capable of bearing more weight.

The kitchen should be placed in the southeast, as this is the direction of the element fire (*agni*). Place windows and doors in the northwest to allow fresh air into your home; this will allow Vastu Purusha to breathe easily. The southwest is where the dæmon's feet lie. This part of the building should be higher than the rest of the house.

The center of the plot relates to the *nabhi* (navel) and, ideally, there shouldn't be anything heavy in this part of the building. The center of a building belongs to Lord Brahma himself, and—in reverence to him—it should be kept clean, open, and level.

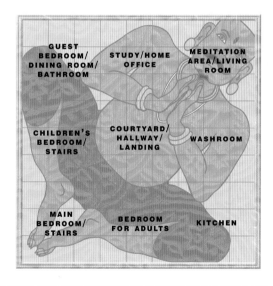

LORD SHIVA *(left)*
In this early southern Indian carving, the lord of creation and destruction is depicted teaching the shastras, *ancient Vedic texts that provide guidelines for the design and construction of towns and buildings.*

A BLUEPRINT FOR THE HOME *(left)*
Each part of Vastu Purusha's figure within the mandala relates to a particular room in the house. For example, the meditation area is ruled by his head.

**THE PECAKA
DIAGRAM**
(right)

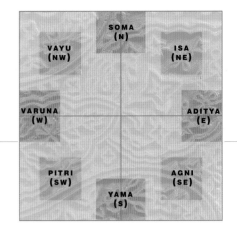

ANCIENT DIAGRAMS

The *shastras* give 32 specific diagrams for the construction of different buildings. Each diagram is suited to a particular site, taking into account the building's use, and they stress the importance of positioning the deities correctly. Deities occupy particular squares, as shown in the diagrams.

1. THE SAKALA DIAGRAM (1 X 1 SQUARE)

This is the simplest of the diagrams and involves only one square. The single room's four walls are at right angles to each other, representing stability and the simplicity of life. Such a house is suitable for sages and for performing *hawans* —ceremonies to honor the ancestors (*pitris*) and the gods. The sacred fire is lit on a square altar in the middle of the room.

2. THE PECAKA DIAGRAM (2 X 2 SQUARES)

Here, the square is subdivided into four squares. These four squares honor the deities Pausaca, Bhuta, Raksas, and Visagraha. This type of building is used for sages and ascetics. In each of the above squares, the sage has to place a figurine, a symbol, or an image of Lord Shiva.

3. THE PITHA DIAGRAM (3 X 3 SQUARES)

This is a square subdivided into nine squares. The four squares in the cardinal directions—north, east, south, and west— symbolize the four Vedas. The four inter-cardinal directions—northeast, southeast, southwest, and northwest—represent the four elements of water, fire, earth, and wind respectively. The center represents the element of space or *akaash*.

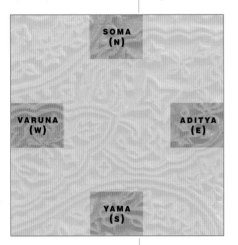

**THE SAKALA
DIAGRAM**
(above)

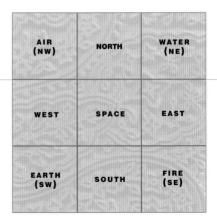

**THE PITHA
DIAGRAM**
(right)

4. THE MAHAPITHA DIAGRAM (4 X 4)

This diagram has 16 squares and 25 deities. Starting from the northeast, in a clockwise direction, the outer ring is occupied by the gods Isa, Jayanta, Aditya, Bhrisa, Agni, Vitatha, Yama, Bhringa, Pitri, Sugriva, Varuna, Sosha, Vayu, Mukhya, Soma, and Aditi. The inner circle is ruled by the deities Apavasta, Aryaman, Savitra, Vivasvat, Indra, Mitra, Rudra, and Bhudhara. Lord Brahma, the creator, occupies the superimposed central space.

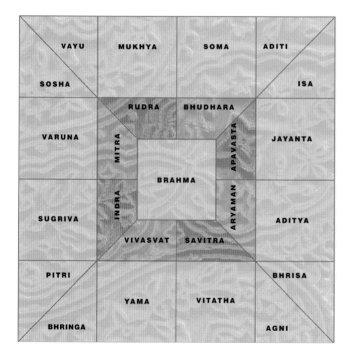

THE MAHAPITHA DIAGRAM (*above*)

TRADITIONAL VASTU

• Build underground water storage, wells, and sumps in the northeast.

• The ideal position for the kitchen is the southeast.

• The master of the house should sleep in the southwest bedroom.

• The north and east should be left open.

• For maximum auspiciousness and stability, the shape of the site and the building should be square or rectangular.

• Position heavy constructions such as stairs and stone pillars in the south and the west.

• The southwest should be higher in plinth level than the rest of the house.

• There should not be any open space to the south or the west of the home.

• Construct the storeroom in the southwest.

• A septic tank should be in the northwest, north, or east. It should not be in the southwest, southeast, or northeast.

• Build stairs in a clockwise direction with an odd number of steps. Such numbers are symbolic of continuity.

• Windows and doors should be in even numbers. Avoid numbers with a zero such as 10, 20, and 30.

vedic *measurements*

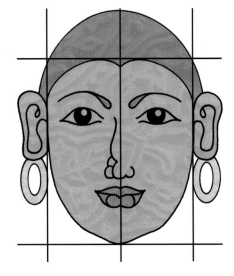

THE FACE *(right)*
The mouth represents the door of the house, the eyes the windows, and the ears the ventilation.

the mouth represents the door, and the eyes, nose, and ears represent windows and ventilators. In a larger context, the person occupying a room has a direct link with it, while the room in turn is directly associated with the house as a whole.

In ancient Vedic times, the *rishis*—ancient sages—devised a system of measurement designed to be in harmony with the laws of nature and the universe. Gradually they developed a set of rules for constructing a temple, a home, or any other building. They considered certain measurements particularly auspicious and established a complex system in which even the mallest of dwellings is related to the entire universe. They drew parallels between the human body and the home—for example,

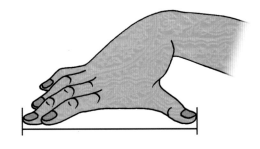

MANA *(above)*
One mana *is the distance between the tip of the middle finger and the tip of the thumb when the hand is stretched out. It is also a handspan.*

According to Hindu mythology, Lord Vishnu measured the earth, the realm of the gods, and the space in between with three steps (*padas*). The Vedic altar consisted of 365 bricks to represent the number of days in a year. They were laid in five layers to symbolize the five seasons and the five elements.

The ancients placed a great deal of importance on the selection of a plot. They believed that, before a building was constructed, the site should be analyzed with regard to its size, shape, location, and orientation. Its surroundings, such as roads, hills, ditches, and vegetation, should also be taken into account.

UNITS OF MEASUREMENT

In Vedic times the units of measurement most commonly used for construction were related to the human body—the width of the middle finger, a hand span, and the length of a forearm. The other commonly used units were the *angula* and the *hasta*. A *yava*—a grain—was adopted as a basic unit of measurement in agricultural communities, about ⅓ inch (7.5mm) long and ⅛ inch (3.75mm) wide.

The atom is the smallest unit both of the Vedic measurement system and of the universe. The *angula* is the smallest unit derived from the human body. Precisely 1⅛ inches (3cm) in length, it is defined as the length of the middle phalanx of the middle finger of the officiating priest. The *angula* is used only to measure the height and width of statues of the gods.

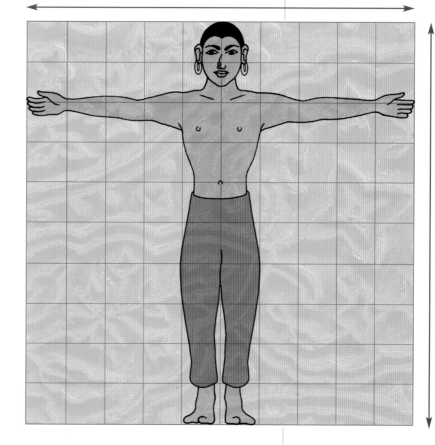

THE BODY AS A MEASURING TOOL

(*above*)

The ancient Vedic sages stated that the width of a human body with arms outstretched equalled the height of the same body from the top of the head to the soles of the feet. Outstretched, the human body fits into a square, mirroring the square mandala used to design the home.

The *hasta* is defined as the distance between the elbow and the tip of the middle finger, the tip of the first finger, or the tip of the little finger. The length of the human body when standing upright with arms held up is considered to be five times the length of the *hasta*. The measurement of *hasta* varies according to the height of the person. Vastu, therefore, tailors the measurements of a house to fit the height and proportions of the owner.

VASTU TOOLS

There are eight tools of measurement: scale or ruler, reference marker, cord or thread, plumb line, compass, leveling instrument, corner square, and eye. The scale (*gaja*) and rope are of standard

THE TOOLS OF MEASUREMENT
(right)

Traditionally, the eight tools of measurement aid the Vastu practitioner in drawing up meticulous plans based on the Vastu Purusha Mandala and the owner of the home.

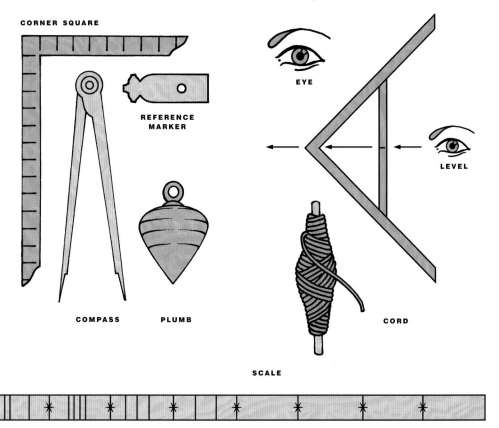

CORNER SQUARE

REFERENCE MARKER

EYE

LEVEL

COMPASS   PLUMB

CORD

SCALE

length and have predetermined measurements. The other instruments are used at the site to draw straight lines and accurate angles for a blueprint and during construction.

THE *AYADI*

The *ayadi* are the formulas for calculating various construction data to ensure that the residents will enjoy good health, good luck, and prosperity. There are six *ayadi* formulas: *aya*, *vyaya*, *raksa*, *yoni*, *vara*, and *tithi* (or *ayadi shadvarga*). According to Vastu, no matter whether one is building a *rajagriha* (palace), a *shala* (humble dwelling), or a *mandir* (temple), the construction should be in perfect harmony with its surroundings and with nature.

 TRADITIONAL VASTU

• Construction work should not be initiated on an inauspicious day. Avoid Sundays, Tuesdays, and Saturdays.

• For the building to be auspicious, the *aya* should be more than the *vyaya* (the length should be more than the width). It should, however, not be more than double the width.

• The house and rooms should be well proportioned. They should not be too long or too wide.

• The height of the building should be in proportion to the length and width of the building.

BUILDING A HOME
(below)
If you intend to plan and build your home from scratch, make sure that you choose an experienced Vastu practitioner to help you select an auspicious site, and create a harmonious home.

choosing *a site*

Whether you are building a house, or buying an existing building, it is vital to examine the site carefully and to consider every aspect before you buy it. Its location, orientation, natural features, soil type, and vegetation are all important.

PRACTICING VASTU *(below)*

Before building begins, a Vastu practitioner gives offerings to the deities and prayers to Vastu Purusha, then decides on the orientation of the house with the help of a shanku or compass. A square or rectangular plot and building is the most auspicious combination of all.

The site of your home should be even, although a gentle slope is acceptable. It should not be low-lying in comparison with the land around it. There should be an abundance of plants, herbs, trees, and ground cover. The ambience should be peaceful and the land fertile. A river in the north, east, or northeast will ensure that the house remains cool in hot weather. And the site should receive enough sunlight in winter to be warm.

Your home should not be next to a highway, at the intersection of four roads, at a T-junction, or on a bend or turn. There should not be any overly large trees in the

vicinity and the shadows of large trees should not fall on the major part of the site between morning and noon. The atmosphere should be clean, unpolluted, and free from traffic noise.

THE SITE'S SHAPE

The shape of the site has an immense influence on the lives of those who will occupy the buildings constructed on it. In a square or a rectangular site the opposite sides are parallel and at right angles to each other. This is auspicious and will bring stability, comfort, and wealth to the owner.

The site of the home is usually determined by the master plan of the city or town. As a result it may be difficult or impossible to find the ideal site. If you have a choice, avoid settling in the heart of the city. A site on the outer edge of the city

may be favorable if it has a clean atmosphere and pleasant surroundings, or choose a site in a rural area.

If you are buying or renting a house, you should ensure that the plan broadly conforms to Vastu principles. You can then make slight alterations and modifications to strengthen the Vastu elements.

AN AUSPICIOUS
TIME TO MOVE?

Vastu is closely connected to astrology (*Jyothisha*) as both are branches of the Vedas. In Hindu astrology, the zodiac (*bhachakra*) is split into twelve houses or *rashis*: *Mesha* (Aries); *Vrishna* (Taurus), *Mithuna* (Gemini), *Karka* (Cancer), *Simha* (Leo), *Kanya* (Virgo), *Tula* (Libra), *Vrishchika* (Scorpio), *Dhanu* (Sagittarius), *Makar* (Capricorn), *Kumbha* (Aquarius), and *Meena* (Pisces). Based on the horoscope of the registered owner of the property, a Vastu practitioner can advise the best time to move into a property or hold a house-blessing ceremony. It is often considered better to move into a property during *Shukla Paksha* when the moon is waxing (the time between a new moon and a full moon).

THE RIGHT SOIL
(*below*)
A Vastu practitioner will test the soil by digging a hole, adding water, and leaving it overnight. The rate of absorption of the water by the next morning will indicate whether the soil drains well or not.

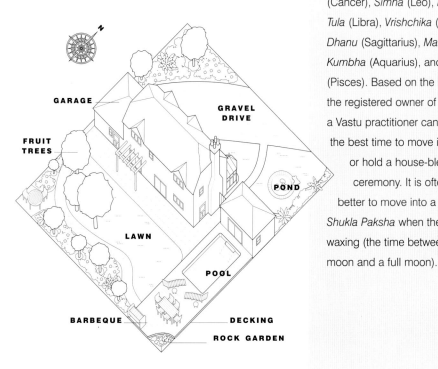

GARAGE

GRAVEL
DRIVE

FRUIT
TREES

POND

LAWN

POOL

BARBEQUE

DECKING

ROCK GARDEN

PLANNING YOUR HOME (*above*)
In Vastu terms, this plan is nearly perfect. With a cleansing pool in the east, a fishpond in the water-dominated northeast, a fiery barbeque in the southeast, and fruit trees in the earth-ruled southwest, the elements are in balance.

THE DEITIES

(from top left, clockwise)

Lord Brahma created the five basic elements out of his own essence. First came space or akaash (opposite page). Each of the remaining four elements need space to exist. Each element is ruled by a deity: Agni is connected to fire; Isa to water; Vayu to air; and Nirritti to earth.

the *elements*

The aim of Vastu is to balance the five natural elements or *maha bhutas*—ether (space), air, fire, water, and earth—to bring health and harmony to home, body, and soul. According to the ancient Indian religious epic the *Mahabharata*, "All things in the universe arising from the five elements are infinite in nature. Even living beings are created from these five elements. The *gati* or movement of anything —animate or inanimate—is due to *vayu* (air). The space or cavity inside a living being is part of ether or *akaash* (space). The warmth of the living body is due to *agni* (fire). The body fluids represent *jal* (water), while the body itself is a part of the element *prithvi* (earth). All living things, including plants, are made of the five elements, which include the five *jananendriyas* (senses)—smell, touch, taste, sight, and hearing."

The theory of the elements was adhered to in the Western world as well: ancient Greek philosophers, Pythagoras and Hippocrates, believed that these five elements made up the primordial energy that pervades the cosmos, the earth, and all living beings. It is now widely accepted that the environment can have a direct effect on one's health. Vastu practitioners aim for a balance of all five elements in the home in order to stimulate all five bodily senses and keep the body and soul harmonious and healthy.

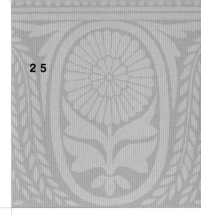

LORD BRAHMA
(left)

Brahma is the lord of the creation in Hindu mythology. He is also the ruler of the element of space or akaash, which was the first of the five elements to be created.

Stars scribble on our eyes the frosty sagas,
The gleaming cantos of unvanquished space.

Hart Crane

"The ether has neither a beginning nor an end. It is a pleasant place where many worlds are situated and even the gods and saints live there, so immaculate is the place."
Mahabharata, Shantiparva

akaash: *the space element*

Akaash (space or ether) symbolizes the cosmic void. According to Hindu mythology, the ether is an endless and remote state inhabited by the gods and *apsaras* (beautiful fairy-like maidens in *Swarga* or heaven). When Lord Brahma created the five basic elements, space came first. All the other elements—fire, water, earth, and wind—require space to exist. Everything, therefore, falls into the domain of this element.

Akaash is also linked to *brahmasthana* —the central space within the home. To create extra space, reduce stress-making clutter by hiding nonessential belongings in chests, closets, and special storage areas.

Although *akaash* is pervasive throughout the entire universe and therefore relates to all directions, it has a special link with the northeast. The northeast aspect of the home should have open space in front of it, and balconies, verandahs, and decks should all face the northeast. The living room, which should be the largest room in the home, should have part of its area in the center and part in the northeast.

Akaash is associated with the sense of hearing. Your entire home should be tranquil and sounds should be pleasing to the ear. Soothing music, played at low volume, will create a relaxed and pleasant atmosphere. External noise, such as traffic, can be muffled with heavy drapes and thick-piled carpets that absorb sound.

QUALITIES AND ASSOCIATIONS OF SPACE

Varna (color):	Not defined		*Guna* (quality): ✗	Bad
Akar (shape):	None		*Disha* (direction): 	Brahmasthana
Swad (taste):	Bitter		*Jnanendri* (sense):	Hearing

BRAHMA, CREATOR OF THE UNIVERSE

According to Hindu mythology, Brahma is the creator of the universe; all forms of life owe their existence to him. He is the most important of the Hindu trinity, which includes Vishnu and Shiva. Brahma is depicted as red in color and sitting on a lotus flower. His four heads represent the Vedas and his four arms represent the cardinal directions. Thus Lord Brahma is the source of wisdom and knowledge. He is kind, just, and all seeing—the epitome of fatherly love. He is very strong, has red eyes, and holds a flag in his hands.

The clarity of space

Space has neither volume, shape, nor color, so Hindus say that the color of *akaash* cannot be defined. In this physical reality that we live in, we cannot avoid selecting one color or another.

People generally choose a neutral palette for the living area, as it is understood to be a restful color scheme. Take it up a notch with light beige or cream walls, natural flooring, wicker furnishings, and muslin drapes—all these will give your living room a light and airy feel, reinforcing the element of space in the home. Glass tables reduce the feeling of bulkiness, and mirrors will further reflect the light around the room. Follow these recommendations

and you will sense the peace in your surroundings and the stresses of the day will melt away.

The diamond is the symbol of space. It also resembles the stars in character and appearance. Like a star, the facets of a diamond reflect the light, and its clarity represents the transparent nature of space.

It works to place diamond and star symbols in those areas of the home that lack *akaash*. Even so, use restraint to maintain an open and calm atmosphere. Too many knickknacks can destroy the feeling of airiness that you are trying to create.

INNER COURTYARD
(right)

The imposing City Palace in Udaipur (The City of Dawn) is the largest palace complex in Rajasthan State, India. An inner courtyard promotes a feeling of spaciousness yet privacy. Similar layouts can also be found in Asian, South American, and Middle Eastern homes.

Of all that is most beauteous—imaged there
In happier beauty; more pellucid streams,
An ampler ether, a diviner air;
And fields invested with purpureal gleams.

William Wordsworth

SPACIOUS LIVING
(left)
The pine-veneered flooring,
woven furniture, glass-topped
table, and light-colored fabrics
all add to the feeling of space
and calm in this living room.

AIRY VERANDAH *(left)*
Muslin drapes accentuate the quality of light and
space by "trapping" the sunlight.

Wild air, world-mothering air,
Nestling me everywhere.

Gerard Manley Hopkins

"Come, O wind, blow healing here, and blow away what disease there is, for thou art all-healing and goes about as the envoy of the gods." Atharvaveda

vayu: *the air element*

Vayu, or air, is part of the atmosphere, which contains all the gases essential for life on earth. *Vayu* cannot be seen but it can be felt and heard. According to the ancient epic, the *Mahabharata*, *vayu* has two important qualities—touch and sound—two of the five *jnanendriya* or senses that need stimulating. The second element to be created by Lord Brahma, after *akaash* or space, *vayu* is necessary for *agni*—the element of fire—to thrive, as air feeds fire.

Water, fire, and wind are the three elements that are always active within the human body. According to the Ayurveda, the ancient Indian system of healing based on the Vedas, these three elements determine our physical and mental qualities in the form of air-dominated *vata* (*prana*, or the essence of life), water-dominated *kapha* (phlegm), and fire-dominated *pitta* (bile). We balance our constitution or *dosha* through dietary habits and lifestyle choices.

Vayu is associated with the northwest direction and is always in motion. This restless quality can be put to practical use. If you do not want your children to watch too much television, place the set in the northwest corner of the room. This will make the children restless and prevent them from sitting still for too long.

If you have guests and do not want them to stay long, put them in a northwest guest bedroom. They will soon have a genuine reason for leaving.

QUALITIES AND ASSOCIATIONS OF AIR

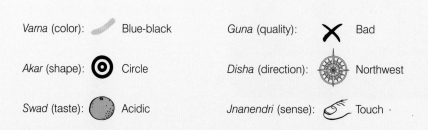

Varna (color): Blue-black

Akar (shape): Circle

Swad (taste): Acidic

Guna (quality): Bad

Disha (direction): Northwest

Jnanendri (sense): Touch

Vayu also activates the powers of thought and encourages progress and achievement of goals. Air and wind are constantly in motion, and therefore stimulate the brain. If you can predict the immediate future, you are under the influence of *vayu*.

VAYU, GOD OF WIND

According to Hindu mythology, air or *vayu* is the breath of Purusha, the supreme being. The deity Vayu is the son-in-law of Tvastra and father of the god Hanuman, who is also known as Pawan Putra. Vayu is extremely strong and very handsome. He is a friend of the god of fire, Agni.

The power of the moon

The wind is associated with clouds and with the moon, which is the symbol of the element *vayu*. According to Hindu mythology the crescent moon decorates the forehead of Lord Shiva. The moon is associated with an alert mind, an ability to appreciate the beauty of the world, and the achievement of enlightenment through meditation. The moon inspires yogis to meditate as they seek illumination and the ultimate truth.

Celebrated by poets for its ethereal beauty, the crescent moon's delicate shape has been compared to bangles or the earrings of a beautiful maiden. In turn the crescent is a popular shape for feminine adornment, such as earrings. The circle is also a symbol of *vayu*. Because it has neither a beginning nor an end, the circle symbolizes the continuity of life, as well as the cycle of life, death, and rebirth.

Vayu has no color of its own, but it is denoted by blue-black to symbolize the sky. It is associated with the sense of taste. If the element of wind or air needs to be boosted in a particular area of the home, hang up wind chimes, hand fans, and flags, or decorative objects and jewelry in the shape of a crescent.

DOME-SHAPED TEMPLE *(right)*
This temple in Karnataka State, southern India, is a perfect example of a dome-shaped building. Many other religions have embraced the dome —one fine example is the Basilica of St. Peter in the Vatican—yet secular buildings like The Capitol in Washington are also undisputed classics.

My soul
Smoothed itself out, a long-cramped scroll
Freshening and fluttering in the wind.

Robert Browning

CRESCENT MOON
(below)

Adding the symbol of the moon to areas that need more of the air element will restore the balance in your home.

LIGHT AND AIR
(left)

This beautiful room is spacious and cooling, precisely because of the open timbers, blue color scheme, and old-fashioned ceiling fan.

Now stir the fire, and close the shutters fast,
Let fall the curtains, wheel the sofa round.

William Cowper

*Absence is to love
what wind is to fire;
It extinguishes the small,
it kindles the great.*

Comte de Bussy-Rabutin

agni: *the fire element*

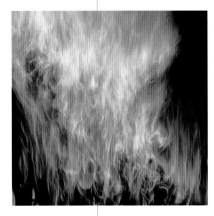

Agni, representing the primordial fire, or life essence, is revered by Hindus and plays a role in life's most important ceremonies. When a baby is born, the family performs a sacred ritual to the god Agni—called a *hawan*—in which sugar, rice, and even lotus petals are thrown into the fire. The fire purifies the house and protects the baby from mishaps and negative influences. During the marriage ceremony the bridal couple take their vows while circling the sacred fire seven times, hand in hand, to ensure lifelong happiness. Finally, when the Hindu dead are cremated, their bodies are given to *Agni*, the sacred fire that embraces all things.

*Agni i*s associated with the southeast—the corner of the home where the kitchen should be located, and where the family meals are prepared. *Agni* is also associated with the sense of sight, and with digestion. The fire element is closely linked with the air element, *vayu,* because fire needs air to survive.

Agni symbolizes the energy of fire and of the sun. It shares not only the heat and vitality of the sun, but also its yellow, orange, and red flames. Just as the sun is the life-giving force on earth, so *agni* is the spark of life in humans.

Fire has the power of transformation. When heated, metal turns to liquid. Wood

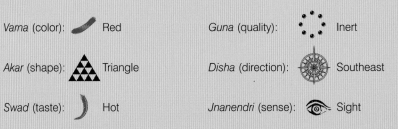

QUALITIES AND ASSOCIATIONS OF FIRE

Varna (color): Red

Akar (shape): Triangle

Swad (taste): Hot

Guna (quality): Inert

Disha (direction): Southeast

Jnanendri (sense): Sight

FIERY SPIRIT
(left)

Agni the god is depicted as the epitome of energy, with glowing skin, and golden hair and beard. Each of his seven tongues—representing the seven rays of the sun (violet, indigo, blue, green, yellow, orange, and red)—has a special name and function.

burns to ashes. There is nothing that is not consumed or transformed by fire.

AGNI, GOD OF FIRE

Agni is also the name given to the god of fire, one of the most ancient and sacred of the Hindu pantheon. The god Agni has three "elemental" forms—sun in heaven, lightning in midair, and fire on earth. He is the mediator between gods and men, and the protector of people and their homes. His three sons, Pavaka, Pavamana, and Suchi, represent Vidyuta (electrical fire), Nirmatya (fire produced by friction), and Suchi (solar flare).

The power of the triangle

Triangles and pyramids are fire symbols. These primordial shapes have great power, and they must be used with care in architectural design.

All commercial buildings rising from a square base to a triangular shape are dynamic in nature. The earth foundation, represented by the square, provides a solid foundation for the upper reaches of the fire triangle. The combination brings stability, success, and fortune. Offices located in such buildings will prosper and businesses will achieve new heights of success in all their activities.

The same principles apply in domestic situations, but they work out differently. A house built on a triangular plot has an excess of the fire element and its inhabitants will face problems as a result. Tempers will flare and residents will argue with one another. If your plot resembles a triangle, you can improve its situation by planting shrubs or trees at the sharp corners (*see right*). This squares off the edges and can create the appearance of a square plot, which in turn will provide stability in family life.

PYRAMID-SHAPED TEMPLE (*right*)

In Asia, temples are often pyramid-shaped, such as this magnificent sun temple at Konarak in Orissa, India. The square base provides stability, while the triangular top creates a powerful place where the gods reside. Other famous examples of pyramid-shaped monuments or buildings are the ancient Egyptian pyramids at Giza and the Mayan temples at Kital in Guatemala.

I crown thee king of intimate delights,
fireside enjoyments,
home-made happiness.

William Cowper

HEARTH AND HOME

(above)

Whether traditional or contemporary, an open fire has
enormous appeal, bringing warmth and comfort to all.

This was among my prayers: a piece of land not so very large, where a garden should be and a spring of everflowing water near the house, and a bit of woodland as well as these.

Horace

"O waters, teeming with medicine, keep my body safe from harm that long I may see the sun." Atharvaveda

jal: *the water element*

Water plays an important role in Hindu myths and religious rituals. Worshippers offer water from a *kalash* (sacred pot) to the sun god at sunrise, whereas priests or *Pujari* offer *charanamrit* (a mixture of *Jangajal*, milk, yogurt, sweetener, and leaves of the *tulsi* basil plant) to worshipers as *prasad* or blessings after prayers. Water covers nearly two-thirds of the earth's surface and is present in varying degrees in the atmosphere. The human body is also two-thirds water.

Water is involved in every function of the body. It helps transport nutrients and waste products in and out of cells; it is necessary for all digestive, absorptive, circulatory, and excretory functions, and we need it to maintain a proper body temperature. If we are deprived of water our bodies cease to function effectively, eventually leading to death. Bathing in water cools and refreshes, washing away stale, negative energies and revitalizing tired bodies and minds. Water in the form of natural waterfalls, reflective lakes, and sparkling streams adds beauty to our lives.

Water is associated with the sense of taste because without it we could not experience sweet, salt, or bitter flavors. It is also linked to the northeast. If you are building a house, it is important to plan your water supply and drainage with Vastu principles in mind. Ideally wells, sumps pumps, and underground water tanks should be located in the northeast.

In the kitchen, place the sink, stored

QUALITIES AND ASSOCIATIONS OF WATER

Varna (color):	White	*Guna* (quality):		Good
Akar (shape):	◐ Semi-Circle	*Disha* (direction):		Northeast
Swad (taste):	Salty	*Jnanendri* (sense):		Taste

LORD OF THE WORLD *(left)*
Isa, the deity ruling water, is depicted as a white figure with three white eyes, riding a bull and holding a trident. As Hinduism evolved, Isa became Rudra, and much later Shiva, the destructive force in the Hindu trinity.

drinking water, and water filter in the northeast. The wastewater should flow out in the northeast direction. A water feature in the northeast corner of a room will encourage prosperity and remove negative energies.

ISA, GOD OF WATER

Isa is lord of the world, as well as lord of the water. Symbolic of purity, he is an incarnation of Lord Shiva and is the benefactor of the world. Isa helped King Bhagiratha bring the holy river Ganga (Ganges) from heaven to earth.

Indoor water features

Water fountains in the home promote good luck, wealth, and prosperity. Ornamental figures and special lighting will enhance this feature. Never place a fountain in the bedroom; sleep is an activity related to the element earth and an excess of water can disturb this balance, and your sleep.

Fish play an important role in Hindu mythology. The first incarnation of Lord Vishnu was a fish. A fish in the form of a boat saved Manu and other living creatures at the time of the final destruction. Fish are also a symbol of Varuna, the god of rivers. Fish are considered sacred, and fish-shaped candy is distributed at festivals and marriage ceremonies. Fish are believed to protect buildings, and in India the entrance to a building often has a twin fish symbol above it. The fish is also symbolic of true love. In India girls often wear earrings and bangles decorated with the figure of a fish. Intricate *kangans* (bangles) ending in twin fish heads are particularly popular.

LUCKY FISH

An aquarium in the northeast part of a room is very auspicious because fish are associated with wealth, achievement, and success. Hindus believe that, if a fish dies despite being well cared for, it has absorbed the bad luck of family members and should immediately be replaced.

REFLECTION OF THE TAJ MAHAL
(right)

The garden of the Taj Mahal, completed in 1654, is a fine example of a garden that is "quartered" by water canals, providing a reflection for this beautiful symbol of everlasting love.

I dreamed that, as I wandered by the way,
Bare winter suddenly was changing to Spring,
And gentle odours led my steps astray,
Mixed with a sound of water's murmuring

Percy Bysshe Shelley

A TIME TO REFLECT *(left)*
The northeast—at the head of Vastu Purusha—is considered to be the source of positive prana or energy. Keep this area as a place in which to reflect or meditate.

PILRIMS BATHING IN THE GANGES *(below left)*
The first Prime Minister of India, Jawaharlal Nehru, once said of the River Ganges: "The Ganga, especially, is the river of India, beloved of her people, round which are intertwined her memories, her hopes and fears, her songs of triumph, her victories, and her defeats."

The thirsty earth soaks up the rain,
And drinks, and gapes for drink again.
The plants suck in the earth, and are
With constant drinking fresh and fair.

Abraham Cowley

O Mother Earth, fill me with that fragrance in plenty, which is there in the herbs, in the waters and in thee, and which is shared by the Gandharvas and Apsaras, let no one ever wish us ill!
Atharvaveda

prithvi: *the earth element*

The goddess Parvati is the mother of the world. She is the female personification of Lord Shiva and is usually depicted with him. Parvati was so fertile that she conceived Ganesh, the elephant-headed god, without the aid of a consort. Parvati is also known as *Kanya*, or Mother Earth. She is the source of all life. Fruits and flowers form part of earth's bounty—a gift from the goddess. To stimulate the earth element in your home, bringing stability to your family, arrange cut flowers in vases and fruit in bowls around your home, and nurture your garden.

The symbol associated with the earth element is the square, or rectangle. It is also associated with the sense of smell —in particular the sweet scent of flowers and ripe fruits.

The earth element is also related to Pitri, the Vedic god of ancestors. All knowledge is an accumulation of what has been learned, discovered, and invented by our ancestors. This knowledge is passed on to us, and will be passed on to those who follow us, through our

teachings, memories, and ultimately—at death—through our reabsorption into the earth (and, some believe, into the collective subconscious).

The earth element governs the southwest direction. If your property has a natural elevation in the southwest, never consider leveling it. The raised section will honor your ancestors and bring wealth and good fortune to your home. Because *prithvi* is the element that brings stability—and to control the influence of Nirritti in the

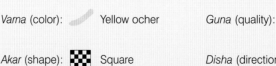

QUALITIES AND ASSOCIATIONS OF EARTH

Varna (color):	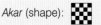 Yellow ocher		*Guna* (quality):	✔ Good
Akar (shape):	▦ Square		*Disha* (direction):	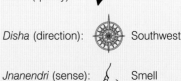 Southwest
Swad (taste):	 Sweet		*Jnanendri* (sense):	👃 Smell

home—place all your storage and heavier items in the southwest part of the house.

NIRRITTI, GOD OF DEATH AND DESTRUCTION

The southwest belongs to Nirritti, who brings misery, pain, and unhappiness to mortals. Death is inextricably linked with the earth element; after death the body is cremated or buried, so it can return to the earth from whence it came. Nirritti is also associated with the dark goddess, Kali, who slays dragons and protects the earth.

Balance and stability

In Vastu, a square or rectangular plot and building is the most auspicious shape for your home. This provides the maximum support, balance, and stability for your family.

Place the main or master bedroom in the southwest corner; it is the area most conducive area to sleep because it is ruled by the stable earth element. However, make sure that your children don't sleep in this corner of the room; they might become too dominant in the family setup.

EARTH COLORS

Orange, ocher, yellow, terra-cotta, and brown are earth colors. Incorporated into the overall décor of the home they promote stability. Shades of orange are subtle and creative. Gold and yellow are uplifting. If red is too strong, cinnamon, mahogany, or maroon provides a romantic ambience in the main bedroom. Upholstery, cushion covers, and bedspreads in earthy or spicy shades provide attractive accents in any room.

SQUARE-SHAPED BUILDING *(right)*

The sixteenth-century royal city of Fatehpur Sikri near Agra in Uttar Pradesh, India, was built predominantly in red sandstone. The Mughal Emperor Akbar planned this city as his capital, but the shortage of water compelled him to abandon it. Today this ghost city has a population of about 30,000, and it still retains many of the old structures, including this splendid square one.

The naked earth is warm with Spring,
And with green grass and bursting trees
Leans to the sun's kiss glorying,
And quivers in the sunny breeze.

Julian Grenfell

HOLY COW *(above)*

The cow is a symbol of the earth element. Just as Mother Earth sustains life, so sacred cows provided milk for the sadhus (sages) and thus were revered by them. According to Hindu mythology, Kamdhenu, a celestial cow, came into being when life was formed from the oceans during the creation of the world.

SPICY SETTING *(above)*

The earthy colors of cinnamon and terra-cotta from the flooring and bedcover add warmth to this traditional Indian bedroom.

vastu *in your home*

Although Vastu derives from ancient Indian *shastras*, its principles are based in common sense and are easy to transfer to modern-day living. It is rare that you will buy a plot of land and build your home from scratch. Most people live in houses and apartments that cannot be structurally altered. However, Vastu provides simple design solutions to change the energy in your home through the correct placement of furniture and the use of auspicious objects and colors.

vastu *and placement*

You may not be able to change the basic structure of your house or apartment, but you can accommodate the principles of Vastu easily into your plans. You won't need to change your personal style, gut your home, or redecorate from scratch, but with simple adjustments you can bring peace and harmony to your family and home.

SIMPLE ADJUSTMENTS *(above)*

If your kitchen does not face the southeast, do not despair. You can boost the fire element that rules the southeast by painting walls, cabinets, or even the refrigerator in fiery colors.

According to Vastu, each area of the home should be designed with its use in mind. Therefore, the main bedroom should be sensuous and the home office mentally stimulating. However, unless your home has been built in line with Vastu principles—where all the rooms will be situated in the directions that rule them—you may consider making some adjustments to your layout. If you are renting, or have a limited budget, you can achieve considerable change through the magic of interior design.

POSITIVE ENERGY

If your home has already been built, it will be next to impossible to alter your floor plan. However, it is possible to bring the positive energy or *prana* into a room by evoking the

element that should rule it. This is simple enough to achieve by adding the colors and symbols associated with the element that should be within the room. For example, if your kitchen is in the north when it should be in the southeast, evoke the fire element that rules the southeast and the kitchen. Paint the kitchen red or orange, add objects in fiery colors, lay down terra-cotta tiles, and decorate with fire symbols such as lanterns,

PLANNING YOUR HOME *(right)*

This floor plan shows the living room in the northeast and the main bedroom in the southwest, in line with Vastu recommendations. However, the fire element in the north-facing kitchen needs a boost—ideally, the kitchen should be placed in the southeast.

KITCHEN

LIVING ROOM

BATHROOM

BEDROOM

MAIN BEDROOM

N

candles, and sun-shaped objects.

Vastu principles are easy to apply to the placement of furniture. The heaviest items, such as beds and cabinets, should always be in the southwest corner of a room, which is ruled by the earth element, and anything to do with electricity should be placed in the fiery southeast.

DINING ROOM/ BATHROOM/ GUEST BEDROOM	STUDY/HOME OFFICE	LIVING ROOM/ MEDITATION AREA
CHILDREN'S BEDROOM/ STAIRS	COURTYARD/ HALLWAY/ FOYER/ LANDING	WASHROOM
MAIN BEDROOM/ STAIRS	SPARE BEDROOM FOR ADULTS	KITCHEN

HARMONIOUS LIVING *(left)*
Space, light, and the liberal use of natural materials bring tranquility to this living room.

AN AUSPICIOUS HOME
An ideal home, based on the Vastu Purusha Mandala:

• The house or apartment should be square or rectangular in shape.
• Have an extension in the northeast.
• The front door should be in the north or east; it is best to have a small porch.
• If possible, there should be an open area in the center of the home, such as a foyer, courtyard, landing, or skylight.
• A living room in the north or northeast.
• A meditation area in the northeast.
• A dining room in the west.
• The kitchen in the southeast.
• A study or home office in the north.
• The main bedroom in the southwest.
• A bedroom for adults in the south.
• The children's room in the west.
• A bathroom in the northwest.
• A washroom in the east.
• A storage area for heavy items in the southwest.
• A safe for valuables in the north.
• A staircase in the west or southwest.

WAX WORKS *(above)*
Candles are perfect in any room in the house. They can boost the fire element in a kitchen, and add atmosphere to a living room, bathroom, or bedroom. Candles can also be used as a meditation tool. However, if you have children or pets, it would be safer to choose colored lightbulbs or fairy lights instead.

VASTU BLUEPRINT *(above)*
You may live in a house with a garden, an apartment with a number of rooms, or even a studio apartment. However, the principles of Vastu remain the same and are based on the square grid of the Vastu Purusha Mandala.

planning *your home*

As you set out to decorate your living space, you may consult a professional designer who is familiar with Vastu principles or you may decide to do it yourself. Plan each room in advance, making sure that all aspects of the design have been taken into account.

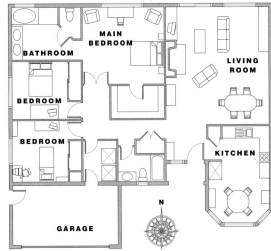

On a separate sheet of paper, draw and cut out furniture templates to scale. You can move the furniture around the plan, taking into account where doors, windows, closets, and drawers need room to open.

Living with clutter is a sure way to add stress to your life, and a clear central space—a *brahmasthana*—is an important concept in Vastu design. A real courtyard is not always achievable, but you can create a symbolic *brahmasthana* to enhance the space element. Keep your

A REALISTIC PLAN *(right)*

It may be difficult to position all the rooms in your home in the most appropriate direction according to the Vastu Purusha Mandala. This plan is almost perfect, apart from the main bedroom which should be located in the southwest. Don't forget that you can balance any negative energy with the careful placement of furniture and accessories.

You will need to assess the available space and then select color, pattern, texture, and lighting to create a particular atmosphere. To design your room, make an accurate floor plan on which you can plot out your furniture and fittings. Mark out to scale, on graph paper, the walls, doors, windows, projections, recesses, radiators, fireplaces, and electrical sockets.

CLEAR THE CLUTTER *(right)*

A clean and tidy home can make all the difference to the atmosphere. Use screens, shelves, cabinets, and closets to hide away the mess of daily life, and you will feel any stress start to melt away.

home tidy and uncluttered. Replace bulky wooden furniture with chairs and tables made of bamboo. Include fitted cabinets and closets, and screens in your plan to keep your house or apartment stress-free.

AN EFFICIENT KITCHEN

The kitchen is one room that needs careful planning to avoid unnecessary stress and use of energy. Follow the "work triangle" shown in the kitchen plan below. Also, keep your dishwasher near the sink, so that all the plumbing is on the same wall. Make sure your refrigerator and stove are not placed next to each other, so that the refrigerator works more efficiently.

 PERFECT YOUR PLAN

• Keep clear "passageways" in a room between the door and the most used pieces of furniture, so that there are no annoying obstructions.

• Position large items first on the plan, as there may be limitations as to where they can be placed.

• Place the television near the electrical outlet to avoid trailing wires, and make sure that there will be no screen glare.

• Take the measurements of the inner edges of doors with you to the store, as well as the furniture measurements, to enable easy fitting.

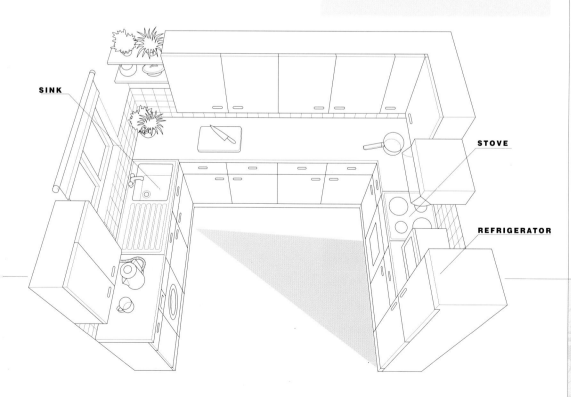

SINK

STOVE

REFRIGERATOR

THE WORK TRIANGLE *(left)*
This plan gives an easy, unobstructed path between the three main activity areas: sink, stove, and refrigerator.

using *color*

Adding color is the simplest and most affordable way to transform a room. Colors are definite forms of energy; they can add warmth or coolness to a particular area and the presence of certain colors can stimulate or soothe our senses. Four out of the five elements in Vastu—and each room in your home—has a color association.

It is easy to enhance an area by painting a room a certain color or adding accents of color. It is not enough, however, just to know which is the most auspicious color for a room. The combination of colors can make or break your scheme. To make the best color choice, it is important to understand the relationship between colors, and how they affect each other.

COLOR IN YOUR HOME *(right)*

In Vastu theory, each element and direction—and therefore each room—is associated with a particular color.

BLUE DINING ROOM/ BATHROOM/ GUEST BEDROOM	YELLOW HOME OFFICE	CREAM/MAUVE/ YELLOW LIVING ROOM/ MEDITATION AREA
MAUVE/ YELLOW/BLUE CHILDREN'S BEDROOM	LIGHT COLORS COURTYARD/ HALLWAY/ FOYER/ LANDING	BLUE/GREEN WASHROOM
RED/OCHER/ CINNAMON/ TERRA-COTTA MAIN BEDROOM	PINK/RED SPARE BEDROOM FOR ADULTS	RED/ORANGE/ YELLOW KITCHEN

USING A COLOR WHEEL

Most color wheels contain numerous complex colors in addition to the twelve primary, secondary, and tertiary colors, providing an extensive range of hues. The main advantage of using a color wheel is that it shows at a glance which colors are harmonious and which are complementary, and whether a color is warm or cool.

The warm colors—such as red and orange—are on the right side of the wheel, and they "advance," making a large area seem smaller. The cool colors—the greens and blues—are on the left side of the wheel; cool colors tend to "recede," and make a space seem larger. The circular design of colors enables you to visually assess the relationship of the hues in the wheel, and to select colors with the desired characteristics for the mood and effect that you want to create.

THE BASIC COLOR WHEEL

Made up of 12 different pure colors, this wheel contains all of the primary, secondary, and tertiary colors. The colors are arranged to show their interrelationship, with the three primary colors being spaced at equal distances apart around the wheel. Each of the three secondary colors is located midway between the two primary colors from which it is derived. Between each primary and secondary color is a tertiary color.

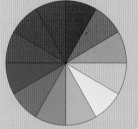

The basic color wheel
This color wheel contains 12 colors. It includes all of the primary, secondary, and tertiary colors.

Primary colors
Red, blue, and yellow are the only three colors that cannot be made by mixing together other colors.

Secondary colors
Violet, green, and orange are the three secondary colors made by evenly mixing two primary colors.

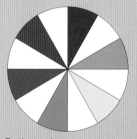

Tertiary colors
These six colors are made by evenly mixing a primary color with a neighboring secondary color.

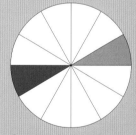

Complementary colors
Colors that lie directly opposite each other on the color wheel are known as complementary colors.

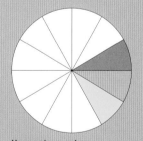

Harmonious colors
Colors that are adjacent on the wheel and share hues in common are known as harmonious colors.

RELAXING COLORS *(above)*

An harmonious (top) or monochrome (bottom) color scheme can be soothing to live with, and is perfect for bedrooms and living rooms.

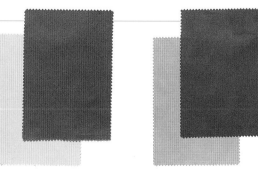

COLOR CONTRASTS *(left)*

Complementary color schemes will result in a strong look, so take care when choosing your color combinations and bear in mind the room's final use.

creating *a scheme*

HARMONIOUS
SCHEME *(below)*

In general, colors that are adjacent on the color wheel result in a restful and easy-to-live-with scheme.

Once you understand the qualities of color, you can start planning your color scheme. Think in terms of the function and design of the space. Consider the effect you want to achieve. Look at the room's proportions and the amount of daylight it receives. Once you have established an overall plan, pick a color that will convey the main effect you want: a cool, spacious feel, or a warm, intimate one. Before you begin, use a mood board to assess and refine your color choice, and to work out which textures and patterns to add to the scheme.

In general, light colors will make a room seem larger, and dark colors will make a room seem smaller. Pastel colors are more relaxing, and bright colors are stimulating.

Many interior designers say that decorating and furnishing a room in a single tint or shade of a color is invariably a mistake, because the characteristics of that color will be overpowering. Overcome monotony by using two or more colors to

COMPLEMENTARY SCHEME
(right)

According to color theory, opposites attract. Here, the combination of orange and blue creates a vibrant look.

provide contrasting hues, or use different shades of one color to provide tonal relief. Highly effective color schemes can be created by using the tonal spectrum of just one color and, when used throughout a room, can create a calming effect. If you are using strong, contrasting colors in even quantities, a narrow band of tones should be used. If the color scheme is monochromatic, or the colors used are harmonious, then a broader range of tones should be used to provide variety.

IN THE MOOD

A mood board will help you assess how well different colors, fabrics, textures, and patterns work together. It is essentially a piece of board upon which you add your paint color swatches, along with samples of carpeting, wallpaper, and fabrics. These boards are easy to assemble and are the best way to avoid making the expensive mistake of buying items that do not fit into your decorative scheme.

COLOR TIPS

• Do not put too many different colors in a room. To create interest, use tints and shades of a smaller palette of colors.

• Pick light, cool colors to make a room look bigger, and use mirrors wherever possible. Choose furnishings that blend in with the color scheme.

• Use dark, warm colors on walls or ceilings to make a room look smaller and more cozy, and pick slightly oversized furniture.

• If your ceiling is too low, use light colors on the floor and ceiling, and darker colors on the walls.

• If your ceiling is too high, choose light, cool shades for the wall and darker colors for the upper areas of the room.

using *texture*

When following the Vastu principles of decoration, it is important to stimulate all five bodily senses to balance the elements in the home. By adding texture to a scheme, you will appeal to your sense of touch as well as sight. Natural materials give a down-to-earth feeling to any décor. Stone, brick, plaster, sisal, and unbleached linen will bring good *prana* or positive energy into your living space.

Materials for building and decorating in the Vastu way should always come from a sustainable source. They should be free from chemical pollutants and be resistant to bacteria, molds, and termites. In addition, they should be durable, long lasting, and easy to maintain.

BRICKS
Bricks are durable, low in cost, and resistant to molds and bacteria—perfect building materials in Vastu terms. They can be used on walls—painted or left bare—or on floors, sealed with boiled linseed oil against stains.

CARPETS AND RUGS
Aside from traditional wool carpets, there are other tactile, natural, and hard-wearing floorings on the market, such as jute, sisal, coir, seagrass, and rush. These

are not usually waterproof, so avoid using them in the bathroom or kitchen. Although they are a good choice for hallways, where there is more human traffic, they are not safe to use on stairs. Ethnic rugs are a good way of adding colorful accents to a monochromatic scheme.

FABRICS
Linen, cotton, silk, velvet, burlap, felt, and wool are all natural fabrics with interesting textures. Layering different tactile elements together—especially in a monochromatic scheme—will give life to your scheme and banish any hint of monotony. Some fabrics, such as glossy silks, reflect the light, and others, such as velvet, soak it up. Choose your fabric to suit your scheme: an opulent chenille throw for coziness or a more rustic airy muslin curtain to let light into a room.

FLOOR TILES

Stone, slate, and ceramic tiles are durable and great for warmer climates. Sandstone, limestone, and terra-cotta are softer and more porous. These softer substances need to be specially sealed to be waterproof and stain-resistant, but they are attractive alternatives to stone, especially in the kitchen. Cork, linoleum, or rubber are much softer underfoot.

PAINTS AND WALLPAPERS

Walls provide an ideal canvas on which to experiment with variations of texture, from rough plaster to special paint effects (see pages 62–65), and there is a wide range of wallpapers on the market to choose from.

WALL TILES

Ceramic tiles are frequently used as wall tiles, as splash-back, or for decorative features in the kitchen and bathroom, and on porches and patios. They are hardwearing, low maintenance, and hygienic. They are available in a wide range of sizes and colors. Ceramic and glass mosaic tiles are also available in strips for easy application.

WICKER, CANE, AND BAMBOO

Light, inexpensive, and wonderfully textural, wicker, cane, and bamboo can be a perfect replacement for dark, heavy furnishings. They can be made into chairs and sofas, and attractive storage boxes. Do not leave these pieces outdoors, as they will get soaked and then rot.

WOOD

Oak, pine, spruce, and maple are all good woods to use for floorboards. Most commercial woods have been chemically treated against molds and termites. An organic option is to use a borax wood impregnation treatment. Veneer flooring is a more economical alternative to traditional floorboards, and can make your home easier to clean. Bamboo is another environmentally friendly alternative to traditional floorboards, and—unlike other veneer floorings—is waterproof and can be used in bathrooms and kitchens. A traditional Vastu practitioner —a *vastushastri*—would ask the gods for permission to cut down the tree, in a special ritual, requesting that the spirits in the tree leave first.

NATURAL MATERIALS
(From top right, counterclockwise)
Bamboo flooring, cotton, composite stone, glass mosaic, plaster, corduroy, marble, sisal, terra-cotta, marble, composite stone, glass mosaic, satin, cork, wool.

lighting *styles*

Light plays an important part in creating an atmosphere in a room and should always be taken into account when planning a new decorating scheme.

In Vastu terms, it is better if light emanates from the north and east, because you will want the positive energy of the northeast to flow into and throughout your home. Illumination can come from windows or

artificial lighting along those walls. Make sure your main source of light does not come from the southeast, because this represents heat and fire.

PART OF YOUR SCHEME

Before buying any lighting, consider how the light will be used. Bathrooms, kitchens, and staircases need strong lighting, whereas bedrooms, living rooms, and dining rooms can take on a more intimate atmosphere with subdued lighting.

Proportions are also a factor: a room with a tall, high ceiling will feel cozier and less imposing if the source of light is

DECORATIVE FLOURISH *(right)*

Create special pools of light with accent lighting, available in a wide variety of styles.

MEDIEVAL MAGIC *(left)*

In a room with a low ceiling, light that shines upward will create a feeling of spaciousness. Here, the mock medieval style creates a warm atmosphere.

SPOTLIGHTS *(below)*

Before choosing your lighting, think how the room will be used. Spotlights are excellent for kitchens, where task lighting is essential.

directed downward; in a room that has a low ceiling, the light should point upward. In rooms without a window, such as a hallway or a bathroom, you might consider installing a skylight or adding a window; also use light-reflecting materials such as high-gloss paint, and glass, metallic, and ceramic surfaces.

With direct sunlight at noon, the colors in a room will retain their original hue. Tungsten lightbulbs will have the effect of warming neutral and pale colors, yet fluorescent and halogen bulbs will drain them (they work best with strong colors). Candlelight and firelight are both soothing and romantic. For a dramatic effect that adds more light to an area, place a line of candles in front of a mirror. If you are unable to use these in your home (if you have children or pets), you can use specially colored lightbulbs or sparkling fairy lights to enhance the atmosphere.

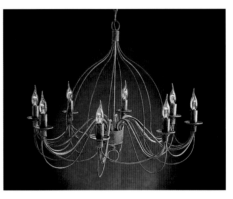

THE RIGHT LIGHT

Ideally, you should use a combination of lighting styles: ambient lighting (pendant or wall lamps, or up- and downlighters to throw light over a large area); task lighting (desk lamps or halogen spotlights for a specific activity, such as cooking or working); and accent lighting (spotlights or picture lights to pick out interesting features such as a painting).

HEAD DOWN *(left)*

Green stimulates mental activity, so this desk lamp would be an appropriate option.

GO LIGHTLY *(left)*

In some rooms—such as the bedroom or dining room—a softer light may be preferable. This chandelier is perfect if you have children or pets, and can't use real candles.

SLICK DESIGN *(above)*

There are many contemporary designs available, such as this sleek metal and glass lamp.

decorate *the vastu way*

If your home does not conform to Vastu principles, or if you are moving into a house with Vastu-related problems, you can take some basic steps to remedy the situation. It is, of course, impossible to change the orientation of a home, but you can help boost its positive *prana*.

Whenever possible, position windows and doors in the north, northeast, or east directions, especially in the morning when positive energy flows into the home. Keep the doors, windows, and other openings in the south, southwest, and west closed most of the time, particularly in the afternoon. This will prevent negative energies from flowing into the house.

Planting all trees in the southwest will symbolically increase the height of the dwelling in this direction, which is important in Vastu design; you can even raise the height of garden walls in the southwest by placing potted plants along them.

MISSING CORNERS

When a house or a room has a missing corner, or is L-shaped, one of the directions is missing, together with its related element. To counter this, you can instal large mirrors at the "L" junction so that the corner looks complete.

When a direction is missing, its related element becomes weak. Strengthen the element by including its color or symbol. For example, if the southeast corner is missing and the fire element is weak, add candles, paint the area red, and use plenty of red accessories. If the northeast corner is missing, and the water element is weak,

BEFORE VASTU *(left)*
This bedroom looks cluttered and unwelcoming, mainly because of the old carpet, the unattractive drapes, the sturdy chest at the end of the bed, and the messy clothes rail.

RUBBER GLOVES

RAGGING PAD

STENCIL PAPER

use white accessories and paintwork, and add water symbols such as an aquarium, a fountain, or a fish-shaped object.

PREPARATION IS KEY

Preparing and planning for any decorating project is vital to ensure that the finish is hard-wearing and attractive. Preparation is always the least appealing part of any decorating project, but it is essential and must be looked on as part of the project.

Plan the order of the work you will be doing before you start decorating. Before painting, tiling, or wallpapering, make sure your furniture and carpets will not be splashed with paint or damaged. If you can, roll up the carpet or cover it with drop cloths, right to the edge of the floor. Wash painted walls, strip off old wallpaper or chip off old tiles, and fill holes or cracks with one of the many types of filler that are widely available. Remember to keep the room well ventilated and always wear a safety mask and glasses.

Special paint effects like colorwashing, rag rolling, ragging, sponging, and stenciling can stimulate the senses of sight and touch—essential to balancing the elements in your home—by adding texture and enhancing color.

BRUSHES

PAINT KETTLE

ROLLER TRAY

SPONGE

AFTER VASTU (right)

A uniform color for the walls and ceiling, and natural wooden flooring give the illusion of space. A new built-in closet clears the room of clutter, and the bulky storage chest is moved elsewhere. Finally, an assortment of textured fabrics on the bed unite this harmonious scheme.

COLORWASHING

Colorwashing is a relatively simple paint effect, using a tinted glaze to produce a restful and textured color tint on a wall surface. Texture is created by the way in which the glaze is applied, and its coarseness depends on how much you soften this application. Colorwashing requires a light-colored base coat of emulsion paint, which works as the background for the glaze. It is a particularly good paint finish for rough or uneven wall surfaces, because the color tends to be picked up more clearly within the grainy texture of such walls.

COLORWASH

(above)

Any washed effect relies on the broken color work for its look, but should also appear neat. To sharpen up the finish another wash layer can be added around the edges to make the paint appear more solid in these parts. Also paint the baseboard and cornice a solid color.

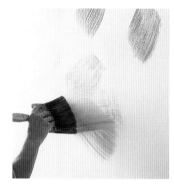

1 . *Dip the tips of your paintbrush into your first colorwash mixture and scrape off the excess on the rim of a pail. Starting in a top corner, apply dabs of the wash to an area of manageable size.*

2 . *While the wash is still wet and without adding any more wash to the brush, immediately brush these dabs out in random directions in large sweeping strokes to join the wash marks together.*

3 . *Move on to an adjacent area. Apply the wash in random dabs and brush it out using sweeping brush strokes, as in steps 1 and 2. Blend the edges of the two areas together with a dry brush.*

4 . *Continue to apply the wash by working in manageable areas. Blend the patches together with a dry brush, holding the brush by the bristles and flicking outward in random directions.*

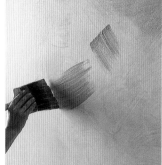

5 . *Dip the tips of a clean paintbrush in the second colorwash mixture and apply dabs of it over the previous wash. Don't follow the pattern of patches used for the first colorwash coat.*

6 . *Without adding any more wash to the brush, use it in sweeping strokes to join the paint patches and create a light all-over finish. Once dry, any thin patches can be brushed over once more.*

RAG ROLLING AND RAGGING

Rag rolling and ragging also uses a tint. This is applied to the wall with a rag or paintbrush, and a rag is then applied or rolled onto the glaze to create patterns or impressions. Although ragging and rag rolling are created in similar ways, the two effects are markedly different. Ragging alone provides a highly textured paint finish, whereas rag rolling turns this finish into a more directional effect, as the rags are rolled down the wall surface in one direction.

1. *Dip the bristles of your paintbrush into the wash mixture. Scrape off the excess on the rim of the pail. Starting in the top corner of the wall, stroke the mixture onto the wall in random directions.*

2. *Immediately, using the same paintbrush, stipple all over the paint mixture in a pouncing motion to remove all traces of the previous brush strokes.*

3. *Again act quickly. Loosely fold a thick cellulose cloth or a chamois leather and dab it over the wet surface. Alternate the angle of the cloth and refold it quite often, to give a varied, natural look.*

4. *The mixture used for the second layer should be slightly thinner than the first. Work the second layer in the same way as the first, using random brush strokes to apply an area of wash.*

5. *Use the same brush to stipple the wash and disguise the previous brush strokes.*

6. *Loosely fold the cloth as before and dab it over the wet wash to remove it in places. Following step 3, continue covering the wall with patches of stippled and ragged wash.*

RAG ROLLING *(above)*
This effect needs to be done quickly, so it can be easier for two people to work at the same time. Always use the same person for brushing on while the other does the ragging, because no two people will do an effect in exactly the same way.

SPONGING

Sponging glaze onto walls is simple and effective. Dip a natural sponge into the glaze, dab it onto a cloth or paper towel to remove the excess, and apply it haphazardly to the wall. Work quickly, and do not press too hard or turn the sponge when it is in contact with the surface. Wash the sponge often to prevent the buildup of glaze.

SPONGING *(above)*

Using the most basic of tools, you can achieve a finish that has depth without being intrusive. The light colors chosen reflect the lightness of touch that is needed to sponge successfully.

1. *Hold your sponge firmly in one hand, pinching out chunks from around the edges and across the flat surface, until the whole area is pitted.*

2. *Pour the paint into a roller tray. Press the sponge into the paint, then dab it over the raised area of the tray to remove any excess. Dab the sponge onto the wall then lift it clean away to avoid smudges.*

3. *Continue sponging all across the wall until the surface is well covered, but the base coat is still visible. Leave the wall to dry thoroughly. Wash out the sponge.*

4. *Pour the second color of paint into a clean roller tray and remove the excess by dabbing it on the flat area of the tray.*

5. *Dab the sponge onto the dry first layer following step 2. Continue across the surface, evenly covering the wall without obliterating the base coat.*

6. *Stand back from the wall to judge the evenness of the effect and apply more paint where needed. Treat the edges and corners as before with a small chunk of sponge.*

STENCILING

Using stencils on both the walls and floors in a room is a simple way of producing a well-integrated scheme. There is a wide range of manufactured stencil designs to choose from, or it can be very rewarding to make your own. Stencils can be made from pieces of thin cardboard or longer-lasting acetate. It is worth experimenting with various colors on some scrap paper so that you are sure of your choice before you start on the wall or floor surface.

1. *Dip the tips of your paintbrush into the paint. Starting in a corner apply dabs of paint to the wall. While the paint is still wet, brush the dabs out in random directions. Blend the edges and leave to dry.*

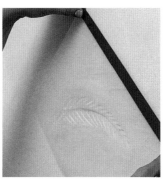

2. *Tear off a length of low-tack masking tape. Press the tape along the top of the stencil. Press the stencil onto the wall in the first, random position.*

3. *Dip the tips of a large fitch brush into the paint and dab off the excess (when stenciling, use paint sparingly). Dab the flat of the brush over the surface of the stencil in a pouncing motion.*

STENCILING
(below)
This is one effect where the surface of the wall must be perfect. If the stencil is painted over any uneven surface, the pattern will distort the surface or bleed under the stencil.

4. *Lift the stencil while it is still fixed to the wall by the tape and check it is evenly covered. Replace the stencil and go over unpainted areas. Peel the stencil back and carefully roll the tape from the wall.*

landscaping *your plot*

Gardens are a private sanctuary, a personal paradise. Plants cleanse the air of pollutants and carbon dioxide. They release life-giving oxygen, comforting moisture, and soothing fragrances. The earth element represents solidity and stability, and creating a garden will link the house directly with this element, bringing stability to everyone who lives there.

GARAGE
FRUIT
TREES

HOUSE

GRAVEL
DRIVE

POND

POOL

OUTDOOR GRILL

ROCK GARDEN

VISUALIZE YOUR PLOT *(above)*

It is useful to draw up a plan to work out your landscape design, before you buy plants or start digging up the soil.

Traditionally, the shape of a garden and the plants and other features in it were true to their local surroundings, as building materials were difficult to transport and the geology of the site had an important role to play. Vastu practitioners still analyze the soil in an area, and follow age-old rituals when choosing a site. The use of natural materials is important. Among conservationists it is now considered ecologically sound to use plants that are native to the local area.

THE MANDALA AND YOUR GARDEN

The garden plot falls into the same celestial design grid as the house: the Vastu Purusha Mandala. It is most auspicious if your garden is square; a rectangle is acceptable, as long as it is not too long and narrow. An irregularly-shaped garden—especially one missing the northeast corner—can be landscaped to square off the corners. Before designing your garden, check the Vastu guidelines for landscaping (see the checklist on page 69), and you will see that the ideas outlined are rooted in common sense.

The boundary of any site is very important; it is effectively the square of the mandala where the dæmon Vastu Purusha is trapped, and the boundary will regulate the flow of positive energy or *prana* into and out of the site. According to Vastu,

TRANQUIL HIDEAWAY *(left)*

Tuck yourself away with a book in a corner of the porch. The stresses of the day will soon melt away among the hanging plants and pots of greenery. Porches can also be used as an informal dining area or as a space for your children to play in.

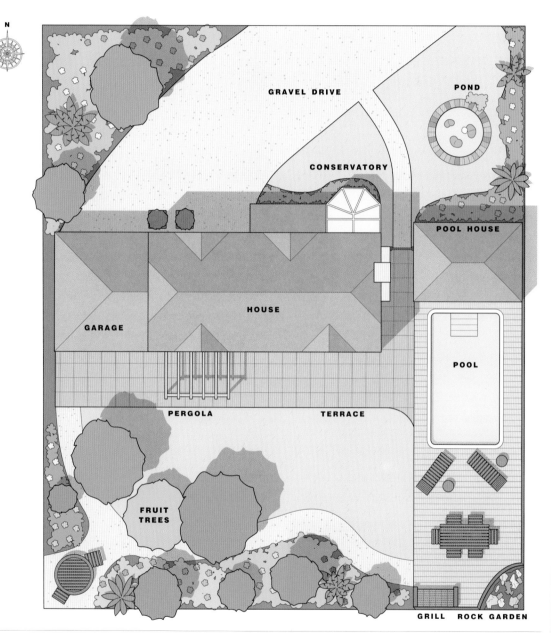

N

GRAVEL DRIVE

POND

CONSERVATORY

POOL HOUSE

GARAGE

HOUSE

POOL

PERGOLA   TERRACE

FRUIT TREES

GRILL   ROCK GARDEN

GROW YOUR OWN
(*above*)
Gardening can be very
therapeutic, whether you are
digging, pruning, potting,
or watering.

THE PERFECT PLOT (*above*)

In Vastu, some objects are best placed in a
specific direction. Plant trees in the south and the
west to stop the positive energy that flows in from
the north and east from escaping. Keep the
outdoor grill in the southeast, which is ruled by fire.

Place water features such as ponds and fountains
in the northeast, to boost the water element.
Swimming pools can also be in the east, as this
direction is associated with bathing. Use natural
materials such as wooden decking or terra-cotta
and stone tiles when landscaping your site.

FLOWING WATER
(above)

Pools and ponds should be placed in the northeast or east. If you have neither, add a small water feature to boost the water element in these areas.

energy flows in from the northeast (where Vastu Purusha's head lies) and exits through the southwest (where his feet are), so the south and west walls of a boundary should be higher than the north and east, to keep the positive energy inside the property. Also, fences with vertical slats obstruct *prana* more effectively than fences with horizontal slats. It is therefore better to have horizontal-slatted fences along the northeast of the property, to allow the flow of *prana* in, and vertical-slatted fences along the southwest to keep the *prana* from flowing out.

REFRESHING WATER

Include a water feature in your garden design—it is written in the ancient Vedic texts that water transforms into *prana* or energy. However, don't place your pond in the southeast corner, as this is ruled by the fire element. If you do happen to have a central courtyard in your house, this is the most auspicious place to have a fountain. In hot, dry countries, a traditional courtyard

with fountain brings a welcome coolness right into the heart of the home.

If you live in a warm climate, and you have the room, an outdoor swimming pool is a wonderful way to keep fit and relax. It should be built where it will catch the sun, and away from trees and falling leaves. Ideally, a pool should be built between the northeast and the east. The benefits of a beautiful pool often far outweigh the time and money spent to maintain it.

A small waterfall in a corner of the garden will soothe and refresh you at the end of a long, tiring day. It should be in the northeast and should consist of several steps. The lower steps should be longer than the upper ones. Stones and boulders that change the direction of the water flow will give the waterfall a more natural appearance, as will decorative plants and ferns. Water symbolizes wealth, so a waterfall in your garden will bring prosperity and good luck. A curved or moon-shaped pond will enhance the flow of polarized energy. Add water lilies to the pond and surround it with a path. Medicinal flowering herbs can be grown on either side of the path.

GREEN AND PLEASANT *(left)*
The feel and fragrance of vibrant flowers and lush foliage stimulate the senses.

A GARDEN IN THE AMBER FORT *(left)*
This beautiful formal garden in the central courtyard of the Amber Fort in Rajasthan, India, shows how the space element or akaash in your environment can be enhanced.

THE IDEAL VASTU PLOT

• Plant bright, colorful flowers in the northern area of your garden as this will attract wealth.

• Remove any dead or dying plants; or this will bring negative *prana* to your home.

• Plant trees in the southern and western borders of your garden, but not too close to the house.

• Put your outdoor grill or barbeque in the southeast part of the garden, which is ruled by the fire element and is therefore the best place for cooking food.

• If you live in a city apartment, plant a window box with fragrant herbs or flowers, and keep indoor plants.

• Keep an open space between the boundary wall and the house on the eastern and northern sides.

• The walls on the east and north should be lower than those in the west and south.

• If the plot slopes, make sure the slope is toward the northeast; because the northeast is governed by water, drainage should flow in this direction.

• Avoid tall trees and heavy structures in the northeast, as these will repel positive cosmic energy and block the light.

• Covered garages and parking areas can be in the northwest. The east is good for open-air parking spaces.

• Do not add adjoining property in the southwest to your existing property.

• The main gate of a southeast-facing house should be in the east and not in the south. The east is ruled by Indra, king of the gods, and a main gate on the eastern side brings wealth, happiness, security, and children. A main gate in the southern portion of the home can be the cause of anxiety and may bring about loss of wealth because the south is ruled by Yama, god of dharma and death.

Mid pleasures and palaces though we may roam,
Be it ever so humble, there's no place like home.

J. H. Payne

EASY LIVING
(right)
*Whatever your personal style,
the Vastu principles outlined in
the shastras can be adapted to
bring harmony to every room in
your house.*

the *directions*

Vastu offers practical guidelines to bring positive energy and harmony into your home and your life. The orientation of the rooms in a home has a direct impact on the positive energy that flows through the building. Depending on their use, certain rooms—like the kitchen—will benefit from sunshine whereas others—like the dining room—will benefit from evening light.

This section outlines the ideal direction for each room in the house, and offers advice on the use of color and the placement of furniture and accessories. The first floor plan in each direction shows the ideal Vastu layout for that orientation. All other plans are based on real homes. Each plan offers advice on the best way to attract positive energy.

In Vastu, the direction that your main entrance faces determines the orientation of your home (if your front door faces north, then you have a north-facing house).

As India is located in the northern hemisphere, the directions proposed in the original Vastu texts are specific to this orientation. If you live in the southern hemisphere, shift the plans 90° to the right (this means that a kitchen that faces southeast in New York should face northeast in Sydney).

PERFECTLY POSITIONED *(left)*

An east-facing home is highly auspicious, and the occupants will be filled with inspiration and enlightenment. All the rooms are perfectly orientated, and positive energy will flow in through the windows and doors in the north and east.

north *direction*

Kubera (the god of wealth) and Soma (the god of liquids) rule the north. Kubera's symbol is the *kumbha* or holy pot, which is believed to contain wealth. According to Hindu mythology, Soma is also associated with health; the fermented juice of the sacred and mysterious psychoactive plant that bears his name was said to cure many diseases and ailments.

A PERFECT PLAN FOR THE NORTH
(right)

The layout of this house is perfectly in line with Vastu principles. The home office faces north and includes a comfortable chair in the northeast for times when you need to relax and reflect.

THE PLANET MERCURY

The north is linked with the planet Budha (Mercury), and represents intelligence and wisdom. According to the *puranas*—ancient Indian verses written in Sanskrit—Mercury was the son of Jupiter and the moon. He had the power to change gender. He was father to some of his children, and mother to others. Those ruled by Mercury are diplomatic and able to deal effectively with bureaucracy.

LUSH LAWNS *(left)*

Lawns will flourish in the northern part of your plot, and a hedge along the northern edge of the lawn is auspicious.

REFLECTIONS *(below)*

Although this plan does not have a separate home office, attract wisdom and wealth into the house by placing an image of Lakshmi or Ganesh on the table near the front door. Put a bench or swing on the porch to encourage relaxed reflection.

including all body fluids as well as running water. Fall also belongs to Mercury.

VEDIC TIMINGS

In India the period between twelve and three in the morning is associated with the north. It is called *Shaant*, the peaceful or restful time. This is when the whole family is safe at home, asleep.

THE NORTH AND YOUR PROPERTY

Plots that have a road to the north are auspicious, and it is important that there be an open space toward the north so that positive energy can flow in.

It is also beneficial to have a river to the north of the house, especially if it can be seen from the home. Water is an indicator of wealth, so the river can attract fortune and wealth into your home.

Herbs will grow in abundance in the northern area of the garden, if that area gets enough sunshine, and their fragrance

SUNFLOWER *(above)*

Lavender, sunflowers, and marigolds will flourish in a north-facing garden.

They have many friends and are good mediators. Mercury governs poetry, writing, advertising, journalism, commerce, and transport. Physically, this planet influences the skin, nose, thorax, tongue, brain, and nervous system, including touch and taste.

The north is also associated with water,

HERBAL REMEDY *(right)*

Place herbs in the north side of your plot and their taste and fragrance will appeal to your senses.

will permeate your home. The northern aspect is also ideal for a lawn, especially if a hedge is grown along the northern boundary wall.

INSIDE YOUR HOME

The northern area of the house should be clean, open, and devoid of clutter, as a mass of items will confuse the energies. Valuables, such as cash or jewelry, should be stored in the north, under the protection of Lord Kubera. Keep your cash box or safe near the south wall, so that it opens in a northern direction. Place your valuables in the western or southern part of a storage cupboard. Clothing and silver should be kept on a lower shelf. The safe or cupboard should not be right up against the wall. Allow some space between them. If valuables are stored in the bedroom, make sure the cupboard is in the southern

SACRED SPACE
(right)

There are a couple of issues that need resolving in this plan. The restroom and stairs should not be in the sacred central space and the kitchen should be in the southeast. Boost the fire element in the kitchen with candles and other fire symbols, and make sure you always keep the bathroom door closed. Try and keep the staircase area as uncluttered as possible, and decorate it with light colors.

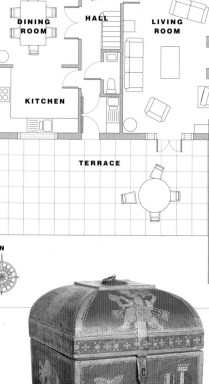

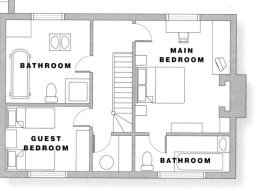

A SAFE PLACE *(left)*

Situated in the north, the office is the best place to store valuables, but keep your safe hidden away in the southern part of the room.

POSITIVELY WELCOMING *(below)*

A north-facing main entrance allows the positive energy that comes from the northeast to flow into your home. Move the desk in the home office so that it faces north, and add pots of green plants that don't require much sunlight.

FRONT DOOR

N

BATHROOM | HALL | KITCHEN

HOME OFFICE

DINING ROOM

MAIN BEDROOM

LIVING ROOM

part of the room and opens to the north. There should also be a window in the north.

A WORKING SCHEME

A home office or study is a very special room. It is here that you can get away to plan, think, read, and write. As Mercury represents intelligence and wisdom, the northern part of your home is the ideal location for your home office. And the Vedic timings associated with the north—those first three peaceful hours of the day—reflect the quiet needed to think

LAKSHMI *(above)*

An image of Lakshmi, the goddess of wealth, is often found in homes and offices. She is an appropriate symbol for a north-facing home office, as this is where you should store your valuables.

MINIMUM FUSS *(left)*

Keep the top of your desk free of clutter and your mind will be clear to concentrate on work.

QUICK CHANGE *(below)*
Turn the desk around so that it faces north. You could also swap positions with the armchair, but avoid having your back to the door, which will subconsciously create tension.

MAXIMIZE YOUR MEMORY *(above)*
A green desk lamp will be mentally stimulating.

A FRESH START *(right)*
The cool yellow of the early sun is the perfect color for a study. Some people find that the early hours of the day are best for work, because they are most conducive to concentration.

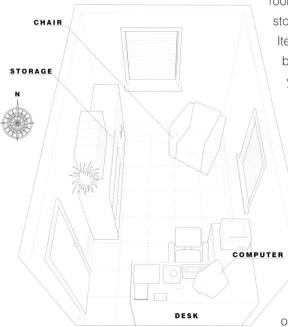

CHAIR

STORAGE

N

COMPUTER

DESK

room to house your equipment and storage, as well as your desk and chair. Items that are constantly in use need to be within easy reach when you are at your desk. Always allow enough space around your furniture to move about with ease.

Avoid clutter on the desk because it can clog your mind, creating negative energy that will be distracting. You could display photographs of loved ones and favorite decorative items on a separate table, bulletin board, or bookcase. The bookcase should be in the southwest of your office, with all your books, files, and portfolios neatly arranged in it, but it should be within easy access, especially if there are books on it that you refer to frequently.

clearly and study efficiently.

When you plan your home office or study, make sure that you have enough

OFFICE EQUIPMENT

According to Vastu principles, your desk should be made of a material such as wood or glass; avoid synthetic materials. The height of your work surface should be 23–28 inches (58–71cm) from the floor. If you use a computer, make sure that the desk is deep enough for both keyboard and monitor to be in front of you rather than to one side, which can cause neck strain. For safety reasons, the viewing distance between your eyes and the screen should be 16–28 inches (41–71cm). You will need to provide sufficient artificial light, such as a desk lamp for task lighting.

Invest in a good adjustable chair that will support your lower back. Remember to leave enough room behind the chair so that you can get in and out easily. Keep filing cabinets in the southeastern part of the room, and your wastepaper basket in the southwestern area.

Working at home can be stressful, not only because of the pressure of the work itself, but also because of the intrusions of the telephone, and even other family members. Keep an area in the northeastern part of your office where you can sit

PLANTING KNOWLEDGE *(above)*

During the day, plants add oxygen to the atmosphere, which will keep you alert while you're working.

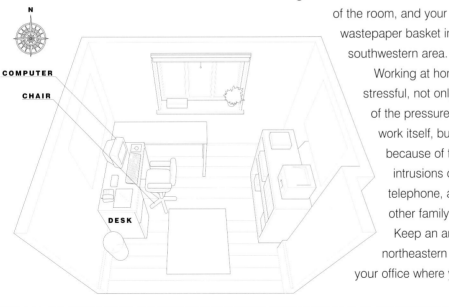

COMPUTER

CHAIR

DESK

GO WEST *(above)*

It would be simple enough to move the storage to the west, which is the most auspicious place for it, and the desk under the window, facing north.

EXTEND YOUR OPTIONS (*below*)
The spare desk in this rectangular home office is useful if you have bulky documents or charts that require extra space. Keep your valuables in the southern part of the main desk or cabinet.

GANESH (*above*)
The elephant-headed god is the son of Shiva and Parvati. He represents wisdom and fortune, and removes obstacles.

and get away from your desk, perhaps an armchair to read in. This way your mind will be a little more refreshed when you step back to your desk.

BRIGHT IDEAS

The ideal color for your home office or study is yellow, as it is mentally stimulating. You may find that a softer yellow is more conducive to thinking; after all, you may be sitting in the room for a number of hours at a time, and bright yellow could be distracting.

Green is the color of Budha or Mercury, the planet that symbolizes intelligence and wisdom, so green objects—a lamp, vase, picture, frame or storage box—will enhance your concentration. Lush green plants placed in clusters in the northern portion of a room or along the northern wall are auspicious and bring good health and wealth.

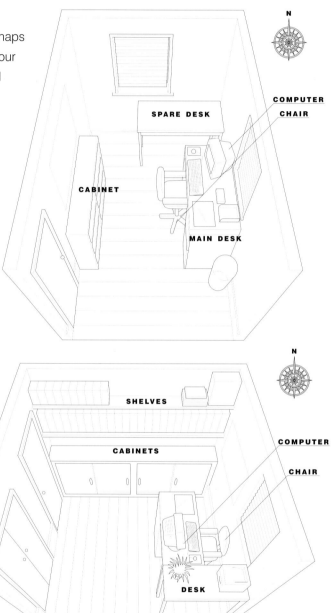

GAIN WISDOM (*above*)
It is better if your desk faces the door, so that you can see who enters. The storage area should be in the south and southwest. However, when you can't easily rearrange the furniture, add symbols of learning and wisdom such as a statue of Ganesh.

VASTU CHECKLIST — NORTH

The best shape for a home office is rectangular or square—use screens or build cupboards to alter the shape of the room if necessary.

The northeast corner of your office is the traditional place for a picture of Saraswati, the goddess of learning, or a small statue of Ganesh, the elephant-headed god of wisdom and fortune, and remover of obstacles. If possible, place your computer or any other electronic equipment in the southeast corner of the office, as this is dominated by the fire element.

The north is symbolic of health and wealth, and its influence can be used to advantage if you have to give a presentation. If you are using a screen and projector, place the screen on the northern wall and block the light from the windows with curtains. Any other display material should be placed along the northern wall.

If your home office doubles as a spare bedroom, make sure that the bed is in the southwest and the desk is in the northeast corner.

Yoga and meditation are excellent stress relievers, so try to take ten minutes away from your desk to relieve your mind and stretch your body.

A CLEAR MIND
(left)
The glass-topped desk gives this office an airy feel, and that—along with the tidy shelves—help to keep a clear mind.

FLOWER POWER *(left)*

Hindu devotees offer fresh flowers and sing aarti *(hymns) to honor the gods.*

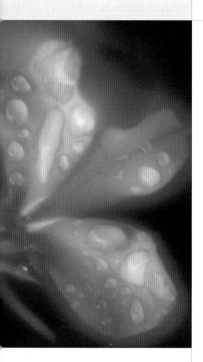

northeast *direction*

According to *Vastu Shastra*, the northeast is the gateway to the heavens and radiates cosmic energy. Since the head of the Vastu Purusha lies in the northeast direction (see page 12), a house without a northeast corner is like a body without a head, and may lead to bad luck and ill fortune. The northeast is associated with water.

The northeast is linked to the planet Brihaspati (Jupiter). Particularly powerful during the day and when the moon is at its fullest, Jupiter is the benefactor of life and protects us from evil. Its season is the cool period between fall and winter. Jupiter symbolizes health, spirituality, knowledge, information, nobility, morality, reliability, devotion, self-control, and long life. Jupiter is associated with the teaching profession, and rules over the ears, intestines, stomach, and feet.

HEALING WATER
(below)

The sound of water trickling over pebbles is very relaxing, and tabletop water features have now become popular.

HOME OFFICE

GUEST BEDROOM

MEDITATION ROOM

CHILD'S BEDROOM

LANDING

BATH ROOM

MAIN BEDROOM

BALCONY

SPARE BEDROOM

NE

LIVING ROOM

DINING AREA

FRONT DOOR

HALL

REST ROOM

BATH ROOM

KITCHEN

A PERFECT PLAN FOR THE NORTHEAST
(above)

The front door opens to the northeast enabling positive energy to enter the house. The living room lies partly over the northeast area and a special meditation area has been created upstairs. Use screens to separate the guest bed from the office area and the dining table from the living room.

RELAXING TIMES *(below)*

This large living room covers much of the northeast, north, and central space. A small area of the room has been set aside as a quiet zone, but some members of the family may prefer to relax on the porch.

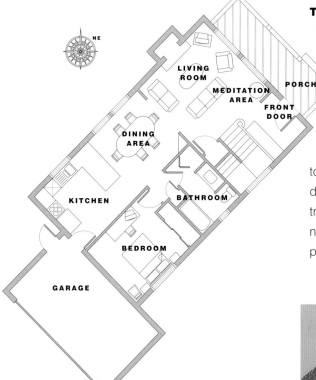

THE NORTHEAST AND YOUR PROPERTY

A small stream or water feature in the northeast of your plot is very auspicious, as this direction is governed by the water element. This is also the reason why, if the ground slopes, it is best that it slopes down toward the northeast; water must always drain in this direction. Don't plant large trees or place heavy structures in the northeast area, as this will repel the positive energy flowing into your home.

CARVED LOTUS PANEL *(above)*

Focus on a favorite image or symbol while meditating to help you push your worries aside.

VEDIC TIMINGS

In India the period between three and six in the morning—when peace and tranquility reign—is called *Brahma Muhurta*. Most people are asleep; only the yogis, *sadhus* (sages), and those who wish to meditate are awake. This is the perfect time for yogic exercises that involve concentration of the mind.

SACRED SANCTUARY *(right)*

This room is a calm, comfortable haven from the stresses of the day; a perfect place to meditate.

HONORING LORD BRAHMA
(right)

The lotus flower is associated with Lord Brahma, the god of creation, and therefore would be the most appropriate flower with which to decorate a statue of him in the living room or meditation area.

HONOR THE NORTHEAST

Hindus often display a figurine of Lord Brahma together with some plants or flowers in the meditation room or living room. You can also honor the northeast by placing a vase of fresh flowers below an open northeast window. Or have a bowl of water with floating petals; this represents the water element and the fresh air blowing in from the northeast will pick up the fragrance of the flowers—stimulating the sense of smell. A small tabletop fountain in the northeast focuses on another of the five senses: listening to flowing water can be very relaxing.

HARMONIOUS LIVING

In ancient times, when Indian homes were constructed according to *Vastu Shastra*, there was always a sacred *brahmasthana* (a central space or courtyard), often called an *angan* or *chowk*. It was open to the sky, and had no pillars or other obstructions. Ideally its doorway was in the northeast. The *angan* was used for family gatherings and prayer meetings to which the neighbors were invited. It was kept immaculately clean and no heavy items were ever stored in it. This kind of spacious construction is seldom

MELODY MAKER
(below)

Music can bring peace and tranquility. It stimulates the sense of hearing, which is important in creating a balance between body and soul.

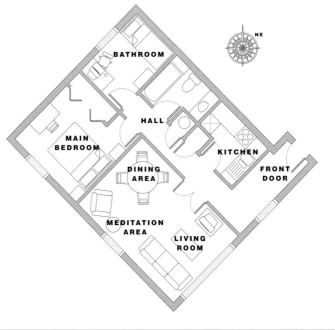

WATER THEME *(above)*

To enhance the water element in the living room, move the television across to the eastern corner and replace it with an aquarium or tabletop fountain. You could also paint the room a light yellow, mauve, or in a neutral palette, as this will increase the feeling of space and airiness.

LIGHT AND AIRY *(right)*

The uncluttered space, neutral colors, and natural materials in this airy living room are perfectly in line with Vastu principles.

possible in modern homes. However, you can still have a room that represents the *brahmasthana*. In most homes, this is the living room. Ideally, it should occupy the center and northeast space of the house, and the door should be to the northeast.

The living room, like the *angan*, is where the family meets, entertains, and relaxes. It should be graceful and harmonious—neither too ornate nor too spartan. The seating should be comfortable and positioned in comfortable clusters to encourage socializing. Flower

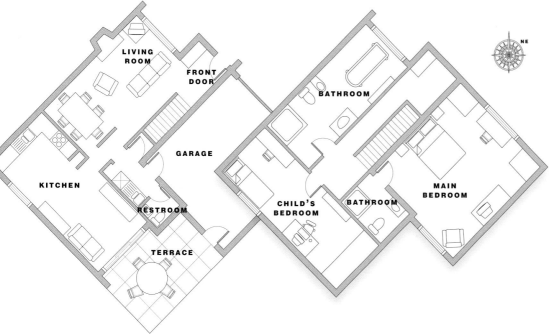

OPEN-PLAN LIVING *(left)*

The front door in this plan opens straight into the living room, giving it a spacious feel. Although this will boost the space element, take care to keep the room tidy and hide any clutter in cabinets, or behind decorative screens. Move the beds to the southern wall, so that the occupants will sleep more deeply.

FISH BOX *(right)*

The northeast is governed by the water element. If you need to boost this element, either add a water feature or position a fish or water symbol nearby.

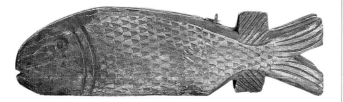

FISHY FRIENDS
(right)
Watching colorful fish swim around an aquarium is very restful.

SIMPLE SOLUTION
(right)
Here, you could move the television into the southeast corner to free up the northeast corner for an aquarium or fish symbol. This will boost the water element in this living room.

arrangements, ornaments, paintings, and family heirlooms will create a warm, welcoming ambience.

If you watch television in your living room, place it in the southeast, as this is ruled by the fire element, which is compatible with electronic equipment. An open fireplace or radiators are best in the southeast area of the room as well. Heavy furniture, such as sofas, bookshelves or built-in cabinets, and plants should be in the southwest area of the room, which is ruled by the earth element. Ideally, there should be more windows on the eastern and northern sides of your room, to let in positive energy. Keep your

living room open, uncluttered, and tidy. Built-in cupboards will hide away essential papers and favorite books, children's toys, and the television and music system, streamlining the look of your room.

Keep the décor in your living room as simple as possible. Light, natural shades work best, and you can add visual interest with textured rugs and cushions, or occasional accents of color. Comfort is paramount. After all, this is where your family will be spending the most relaxing part of their day. Make sure you have enough seating for everyone, so people aren't too cramped.

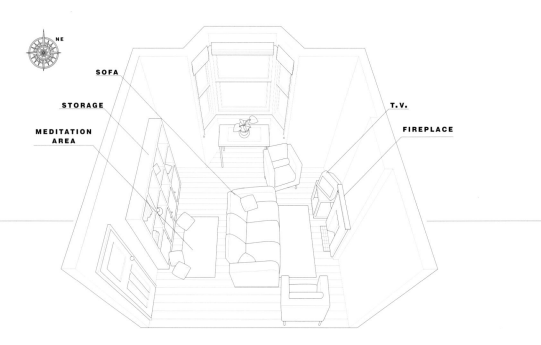

REGAIN YOUR ENERGY *(below)*

Sink into a comfortable sofa at the end of a hard day and take some time to de-stress. Replace the lamp in the northeast corner with a water feature to cancel any negative energy from the solid bookcase and east-facing television.

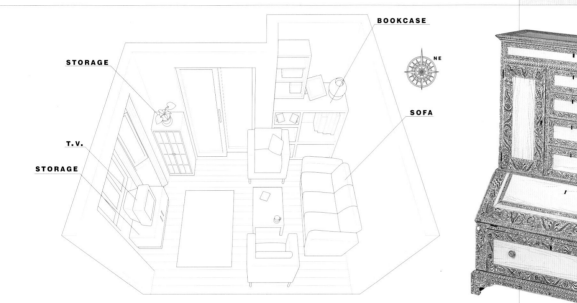

STORAGE
BOOKCASE
NE
SOFA
T.V.
STORAGE

INNER PEACE

In India, many families have a meditation or prayer room or a corner in a room set aside for prayers. This idea can be adopted by setting aside a particular room, or portion of a room, for prayer, meditation, or just sitting peacefully. Ideally this room should be in the northeast sector of the home, because this promotes the spiritual union of the soul with God.

If possible, the roof should be dome-shaped, like that of a temple or church, or pyramid-shaped. Hindus believe that waves of positive energy originate from the highest point of the roof, at the center, and flow into the room. This positive energy promotes inner peace and helps eradicate illness.

There should be no photographs of ancestors on the walls of the prayer room. *Almirahs* (closets) and boxes storing items

TIDY UP *(above)*

Hide your clutter in a cabinet that will match your Vastu-inspired neutral palette.

SPACIOUS LIVING *(right)*

Have as many windows in the northeast of your home as you can, as this is where the positive energy flows into your home. The lack of drapes and clutter will make the room look bigger.

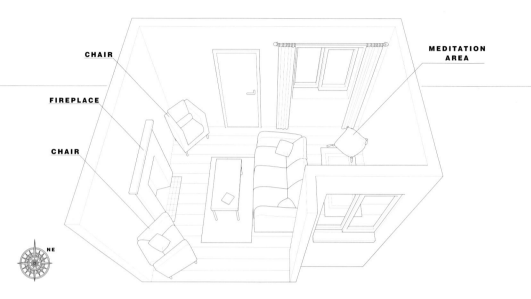

Zone of Tranquility
(right)

If you are short on space and wish to meditate, roll out a rug or mat in the northeast area of your living room.

Scented flowers
(above)

Fragrance is an important part of a room's ambience.

Sociable seating
(right)

Group your sofas and chairs together to encourage relaxed conversation.

required for prayer, such as prayer books, should be placed along the southern or western walls of the room. The prayer room should always be clean and free of clutter, particularly in the central area. It is acceptable to cover the floor with a rug or carpet. Make sure no one wears shoes into the prayer room. Hindu devotees light incense before the figures of the gods every day. They also offer fresh flowers and sing *aarti* (hymns) to honor them.

If it is not possible to set aside a whole room, you can make the northeast corner of the living room into an area for prayer.

Paint your meditation room in light shades of yellow or violet because these colors encourage spirituality, meditation, and prayer. Keep the room as free as possible from heavy items or electronic equipment. This area should be as tranquil and uncluttered as you wish your mind to become.

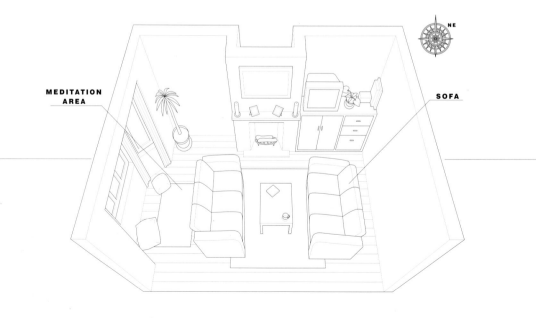

VASTU CHECKLIST — NORTHEAST

As much air and light should flow into the northeast as possible—this is where the positive energy enters your home—so the way you cover your windows is very important. Instead of heavy drapes or shutters, try to keep your drapes light and flowing, or use adjustable blinds, so that air and energy can flow freely.

Never put tall or heavy objects in the northeast because they will block the flow of energy. A shed, for example, should never be in the northeast; it will block the energy flow and may cause ill health and financial loss.

Do not have a prayer corner in the bedroom, as spirituality and sensuality must not be mixed.

The *tumbe* flower (a gourd) is sacred to Lord Shiva.

It is considered beneficial when grown in the northeast part of the garden, together with other medicinal herbs such as thyme and mint.

Kitchen sinks should be placed in the northeast, because this area is ruled by the water element.

If it is possible, put a water feature such as a fountain or fish pool in the northeast; it will encourage a tranquil atmosphere.

TRANQUIL SCENE
(above)
A water feature in the northeast corner of your home or yard will enhance the water element that presides over this area.

HANGING AROUND
(left)
Whether you have a special room in which to meditate, or even just the northeast corner of a light and airy room, take some time out in the day to refresh your mind, body, and spirit.

east *direction*

Without the sun there would be no life on earth, and because the sun rises in the east, this is a very important direction. The east is associated with the summer season, and it is represented by abundant flowers and fruits.

A PERFECT PLAN FOR THE EAST
(right)

An east-facing home will bring inspiration and enlightenment to its occupants, as it benefits from the early morning sunshine. In India, bathing is considered a sacred ritual, and the perfect way to start the day. Here, the bathroom faces east.

GODS OF THE EAST

The chief god of the east is Indra, the lord of heaven. According to the ancient Indian verses—the *puranas*—Indra is the son of Kashyap. He married Sachi, the daughter of a dæmon called Puloman. Indra rules over *swarga* (the abode of the gods) and

ORBS OF SUNSHINE *(right)*

Smell, taste, and touch ripe vitamin-filled fruit, and benefit from the sun's energy.

all celestial bodies are under his jurisdiction.

Indra represents the power of the human mind. All intelligence comes from the awakening of the mind; hence Indra is the bestower of intelligence. When the mind (*mana*) is under control and seeks the ultimate truth, enlightenment comes from within, illuminates the self, and becomes one with God. Indra also represents enlightenment.

The east is also associated with Surya, the sun god. He is depicted with a stout but muscular body and a dark complexion. He is fiery, hot-tempered, arrogant, proud, and daring. His strength increases as the day advances, reaching its peak at noon.

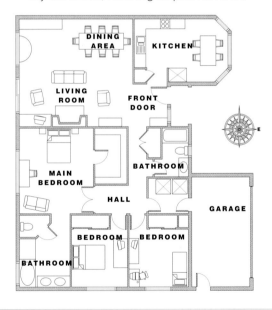

Surya influences the heart, eyes, brain, and spleen. Too much or too little can cause diseases, such as high blood pressure, fever, and disorders of the eye, ear, nose, throat, and brain. Surya rules the head and is associated with strong bones (constitution) and a reliable character. He is also linked with willpower, courage, energy, and health.

Rubies (*manik*) are symbolic of the sun as well as the east. They bring fire and passion into life. Any jewelry with rubies will warm the body and the heart.

MAGICAL MOSAIC (*above*)

The design of this bathroom is reminiscent of swimming pools and public baths in exotic locations.

EASTERN CALM (*above*)

Here, a small bathroom opposite the main bedroom is perfectly situated facing east. You must keep the bathroom door closed at all times, to avoid the spread of negative energy.

MORNING GLORY (*below*)

The bathroom window faces east to catch the rays of the morning sun. Reduce negative energy in the central space by keeping the restroom door closed and decorating the staircase in light colors.

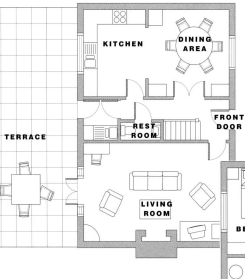

VEDIC TIMINGS

In India, between three and six in the morning, the east is neither light nor dark. Between six and nine, the sun rises and the east becomes *dipta* (lit). Between nine and twelve, the sun radiates maximum heat. From noon onward, the heat of the sun slowly

decreases. The sun becomes increasingly tranquil as night approaches. The eastern sector of the house should be the lowest part of the home, so that it will benefit from the morning sun. This is the time to cleanse your body with water energized by the sun. For this reason, it is beneficial for the bathroom to be in the east.

BIG CHANGE

(*below*)

You can change a bedroom in the east of your house into a large family bathroom, with a traditional free-standing tub and a state-of-the-art corner shower.

THE EAST AND YOUR PROPERTY

The east should be kept as clear as possible to allow positive energy into your home. There should be an open space between the boundary wall and the house on the eastern and northern sides. The boundary walls on the east and north should be lower than those in the west and south.

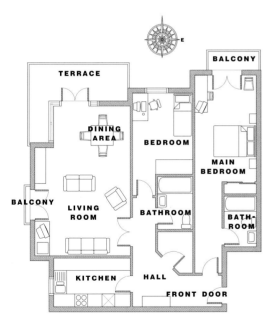

A SACRED RITUAL

The bathroom is not just a place to get clean. A bath is a sacred activity that purifies the body, the mind, and the soul. In India, it is customary to chant *shlokas* (a Hindu hymn or verse) and to recite the name of the *Ishta deva* (god in whom one has faith, favorite god) while pouring water over the body. A deep, warm bath with aromatherapy oils is considered one of the most relaxing ways of unwinding after a stressful day. Keep any candles in the southeast corner of the bathroom, which is ruled by the fire element, and make sure you play some soft, soothing music. These will stimulate four senses—touch, smell, sight, and hearing—bringing your mind, body, and soul back into balance. On the other hand, an early morning brisk shower is an invigorating way to start the day.

FANCY TRIMMINGS
(left)
Discover your creative streak by designing a unique mosaic splash-back above the sink.

SEA DREAMS
(above)
A conch shell is an auspicious symbol in Vastu literature, representing victory and timelessness. Although these shells should never be removed from their natural habitat, it is possible to buy them from reputable suppliers.

KEEP IT SIMPLE *(above)*
This layout looks cramped because the central space is cluttered with doors and rooms. To counteract this, keep the colors neutral throughout and keep the area tidy. Always keep the door shut between the main bedroom and bathroom.

SUN SEEKER *(below)*

The shower is the heaviest object in this room and ideally should sit in the southwest. Enhance the positive energy in this room with the color blue or green.

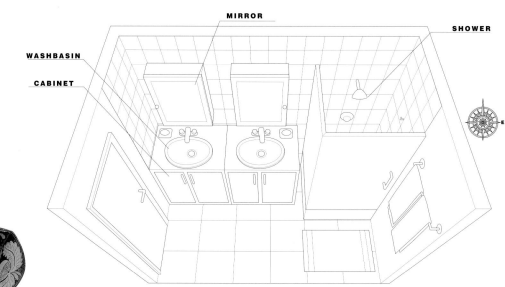

SOAP DISH *(below)*

Decorate your bathroom with unusual accessories found on your travels.

A CLEANSING PLACE

In some countries or cultures, bathrooms without a toilet are common. If you have the space in your home, don't have a toilet in the bathroom in the east; a toilet here would encourage negative energy in an area where positive energy should flow into the house. Preferably, the toilet should be in the northwest. If you cannot have your toilet in the northwest, make sure you keep the toilet lid down and the door shut to halt the spread of any negativity.

Take care to place the bathtub or the shower in the southwest, as these will be

STEPPING UP *(left)*

The architectural design of the tub and the abundance of light that pours into this room would brighten anyone's morning.

the heaviest items in the room.

Reflective surfaces such as mirrors or glass should be on the north or east walls. These will help to bring light into the room, especially if you do not have a window or privacy demands that it be covered up. Make sure you have an exhaust fan to prevent damp and mold, especially if there is no natural ventilation.

WALLS AND FLOORS

Practicality is the key when you are choosing wallcoverings and flooring for your bathroom. Wall treatments should be easy to clean and able to withstand the hot, steamy atmosphere. Paint is the easiest and most affordable option, but you need a silk or eggshell finish to withstand the condensation.

Ceramic, glass, or mosaic tiles provide a good waterproof surface for walls, or they can be used in smaller amounts as splash-backs around the tub and washbasin. Tongue-and-groove paneling is another good-looking choice and can be painted or treated with varnish, and

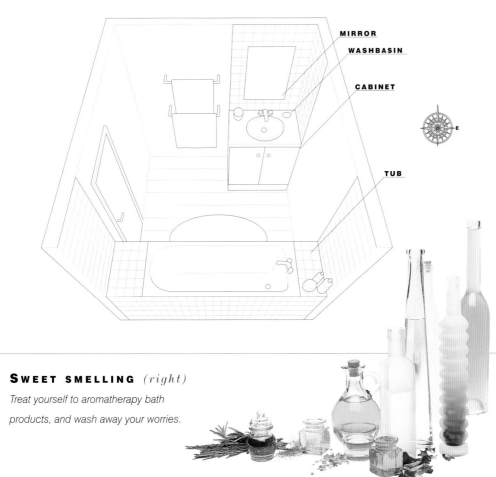

MIRROR

WASHBASIN

CABINET

TUB

E

STEAMY STUFF
(left)
The layout of this bathroom with its heavy tub in the south is perfect for an east-facing room. As this room has no window, install an exhaust fan to rid the room of steam.

SWEET SMELLING *(right)*
Treat yourself to aromatherapy bath products, and wash away your worries.

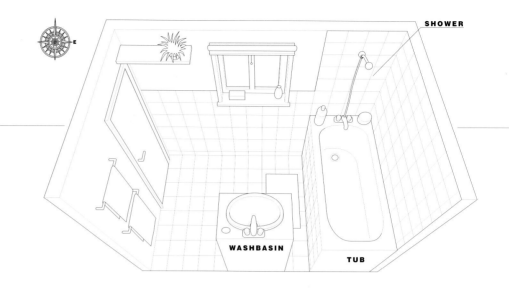

SHOWER

WASHBASIN

TUB

RUBBING SHOULDERS *(above)*

Use natural materials wherever you can.

ALTER THE ENERGY *(top right)*

Replace the plant with sun symbols and paint the room blue to compensate for the heavy tub in the northeast.

PERFECT PLAN *(right)*

This is a lovely set-up with the tub in the west and the "his and hers" washbasins.

bare plaster sealed with a matte varnish has a warm, rustic quality.

For floors, choose moisture-proof materials such as cork or cushioned vinyl, rather than carpet, which can quickly show water stains and may rot. Some synthetic, foam-backed carpets and carpet tiles are specifically intended for bathroom use, but make sure that they can be lifted up easily to dry if necessary. A non-slip rug or bathmat placed next to the bath or shower will provide warmth underfoot and help to absorb any splashes. If you are combining a bath and shower, choose a wide, flat-bottomed bath with a non-slip surface; a

glass bath screen must be shatterproof. Otherwise, attractive plastic shower curtains are widely available and can be wiped down or replaced easily.

THE BIG BLUE

Various shades of blue or blue-green are ideal colors for the bathroom, in Vastu terms, and many people already veer naturally toward these classic bathroom colors. Whether your look is traditional wood paneling or contemporary chrome and glass, good lighting and an easy-to-maintain design are fundamental to an attractive, functional bathroom.

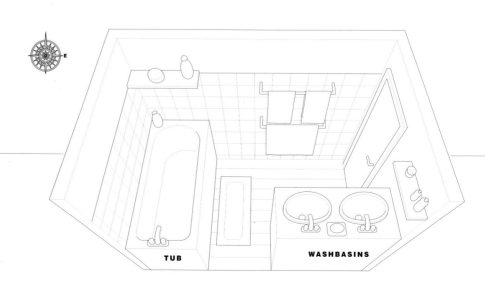

TUB

WASHBASINS

VASTU CHECKLIST — EAST

According to Hindu tradition, the east is important for the sons of the family and is known as *pitristhan* (the paternal place). Traditionally, a male child born in an east-facing room will remain faithful and devoted to his parents until their death.

An east-facing house is very auspicious; it brings wealth, prosperity, and success.

As many doors and windows as possible should face toward the east (as well as the north and the northeast).

Don't obstruct the flow of energy, so keep the east neat, clean, and free of clutter. Avoid pillars, stones, or boulders in this area.

The eastern and northern sides should be the lowest parts of the house.

Open-air parking should be in the eastern sector of the plot.

Do not place flowerpots on top of walls on the eastern side because they will hinder the flow of positive energy.

The roof of a veranda or deck on the eastern side should be lower than the roof over the house, and the plot of land should be lowest in the east or the northeast corner to allow water to drain away easily.

Storerooms and attics should not be in the east, but the southwest.

FIERY FLOWER
(above)
Place sculptural blooms in uncluttered corners of your home.

MIRROR, MIRROR
(left)
The reflective mirrors are an effective way of bringing more light into this contemporary-style blue bathroom.

southeast *direction*

The meeting point of the south and the east is known as Agneya (southeast). The presiding deities of the southeast are Agni, the god of fire, and the goddess Vidari. The southeast direction is Rajasic and is associated with diamonds and with Shukra.

Shukra, the planet Venus, presides over the sensual side of our nature, and represents virility, potency, marital happiness, and fragrance. It is connected to Kamadeva, the Indian god of love, and therefore governs romance, courtship, love, marriage, art, music, dancing, decorations, ornaments, and luxuries.

The planet controls the sex organs, bowel function, and hair. If it becomes a

STENCILED CABINETS (*above*)
To personalize your décor, try some decorative paint effects like the ones shown on pages 62–65.

SOME LIKE IT HOT (*below*)
Fiery chiles and peppers complement the colorful plate and tablecloth.

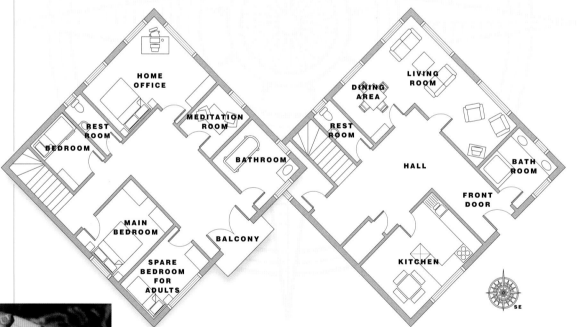

A PERFECT PLAN FOR THE SOUTHEAST (*above*)
In this plan, the kitchen is auspiciously placed in the southeast. To cool the fire element on the top floor of the house, a balcony has been installed to let in light, air, and positive prana.

STOKE THE FIRE *(below)*

Move the television to the southeast corner of the living room and boost the fire element in the kitchen by painting the walls or cabinet doors red or orange.

FLICKERING FLAMES *(above)*

Candles will enhance the fire element in your kitchen.

are sometimes unavoidable. In this case certain factors should be borne in mind.

As a general rule, any home extension should be square or rectangular to reinforce stability in the home. Never build a triangular-shaped extension, symbolic of the fire element. Building an extension on the southeast corner of your home is not auspicious from a Vastu point of view. This will cause the fire element to become dominant in the building, burning up the inhabitants' earnings and causing financial and emotional setbacks. If the southeast corner of your home juts out prominently it may already be exercising negative effects. You can mitigate these and reduce the influence of fire by "rounding off" the outside corners, perhaps

negative force, it can cause infidelity, sexual problems, and diseases of the eye and nose. It can also lead to a shortage of vital fluids and in extreme cases to renal failure.

THE SOUTHEAST AND YOUR PROPERTY

The principles of Vastu do not normally encourage the building of home extensions, but for practical reasons these

SLEEK AND STYLISH *(right)*

The clean lines of this contemporary kitchen, the storage jars, and the "work triangle" of sink, refrigerator, and stove make this a good working space for the cook of the family.

HARNESSING ENERGY *(below)*
Placing fire symbols such as candles, sun-shaped mirrors, and terra-cotta plant pots in the southeast corners of the north-facing kitchen and the living room will bring positive energy to the inhabitants.

GARAGE

KITCHEN

DINING AREA

MAIN BEDROOM

SE

LIVING ROOM

TERRACE

FRONT DOOR

FLORAL BOOST
(above)

Bold orange and yellow flowers will increase the fire element—and consequently the positive energy—in a kitchen that is inauspiciously positioned.

by planting some shrubs or erecting a low rounded wall.

Even more problematic in Vastu terms is an extension facing due south, which can give rise to worries and fears, and ultimately to ill health. If you have a south-facing extension, any potentially harmful effects can be lessened by introducing some form of separation from the main house. Ideally a complete separation of exterior walls is best, but a change of levels—or even some double doors between the main building and extension—will prove reasonably effective.

It is not advisable to remove the southeast corner of a building during alteration works. Not only will this spoil its shape and symmetry, but it also causes a weakening of the fire element in your home that can lead to maintenance problems. If your home already has a "cut-off" corner, you can restore the fire energy by placing fire-related objects, such as candles and lights, in the southeast of your home.

Another way to counteract any negative influences is to install a fountain or other water feature at the northeast corner of your home, either inside or outside. This encourages an influx of northeast energies that will cancel out the excess of the fire element in the southeast. If you live in an apartment without a garden, a tabletop fountain will do just as well.

ALL FIRED UP *(left)*

This traditional Japanese-style wood-burning fire pit is a sociable alternative to a stove, and honors the fire god Agni, who rules the kitchen.

A MODERN COOK
(left)

The chrome chairs, sparkling lighting, and sleek refrigerator set off the wood in this modern scheme, and prevent it from becoming overpowering.

VEDIC TIMINGS

Between nine and twelve in the morning, the southeast is *dipta* (lit and heated). This means that this is the ideal time to prepare a meal.

THE HEART OF THE HOUSE

The southeast is the fire corner of the house. It is ideal for activities such as cooking and eating, which involve heat and electrical appliances, and is the perfect location for the kitchen.

In houses with more than one floor, the kitchen should be built on the lowest level. It should be located away from the main door and be well ventilated, preferably with a fan or electric chimney, so that cooking smells do not permeate adjoining rooms.

Your kitchen may already be situated in the southeast. If so, plant some herbs in

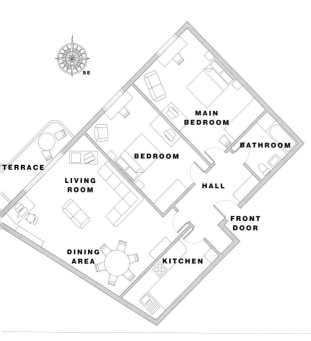

LONG AND LEAN *(above)*

This narrow southeast kitchen is in the perfect position on the floor plan. However, it is long and narrow, so more than two people will be a crowd. Keep equipment in cabinets to minimize clutter.

POTS OF HERBS
(left)

If you don't have a garden, plant herbs in terra-cotta plant pots and keep them on the kitchen windowsill.

CHIMNEY COOKING *(below)*

An outdoor grill or cooking chimney is another way to cook delicious meals, and can be a great reason to eat outdoors. Make sure it is placed in the southeast corner of your yard.

earthenware pots just outside the kitchen door or in a window box, to make a small kitchen garden. The fragrance of mint, rosemary, basil, and lemongrass wafting into the room will enhance the senses.

Eat your food away from the cooking and preparation areas, to avoid any distracting cooking mess. If you don't have a separate dining room, put your table in the center of the kitchen or in the southwest corner.

WORKING YOUR SPACE

Make sure that the layout of your kitchen follows the "work triangle" design described on page 51. You should have

NATURE'S GIFT
(below)

Bring positive energy to your kitchen table with fire-colored place mats, flowers, and fruits.

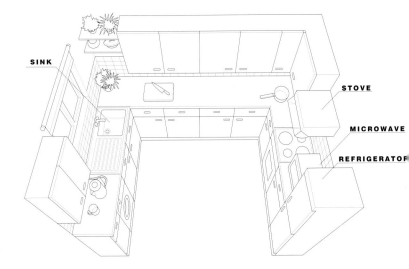

SE

SINK

STOVE

MICROWAVE

REFRIGERATOR

BLOWING HOT AND COLD
(above)

Ideally, the stove or microwave should be situated in the southeast, which is ruled by the fire element. Do make sure that the stove and refrigerator are not next to each other, or they will not function efficiently.

SUN-FILLED ORANGES
(left)

Orange-colored fruit will do wonders to boost your levels of vitamin C.

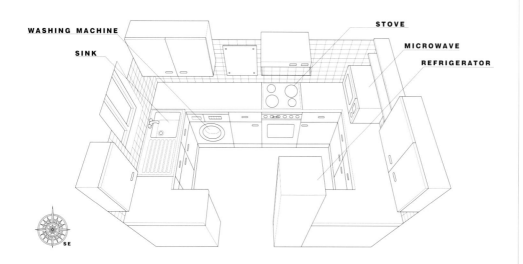

WASHING MACHINE

SINK

STOVE

MICROWAVE

REFRIGERATOR

SE

BEHIND YOU *(left)*

If you work at the stove in this kitchen, you will have your back to the door. Place a mirror near the stove so that you can see at once if anyone enters the room. The refrigerator is run by electricity, so the southeast is a good place for it. Move the microwave into the southeast corner.

an unobstructed path between your three main activity areas: sink, stove, and refrigerator. If your kitchen is not in the southeast of your home, make sure at least that your stove or microwave is located in the southeast of the kitchen. Arrange the layout so that you face east when you prepare and cook food. Always keep your preparation surface as clean and free from clutter as possible—this makes for good hygiene, as well as good Vastu. Plan your storage, work surfaces, and appliances according to where you use them in the following sequence: "store, prepare, cook, wash, serve, store." This will reduce the amount of energy you use rushing backward and forth to

NATURE'S GIFT *(right)*

Use natural materials as much as possible in your home, like this rectangular wooden kitchen table and stools. Note the red flowers, enhancing the fire element in this room.

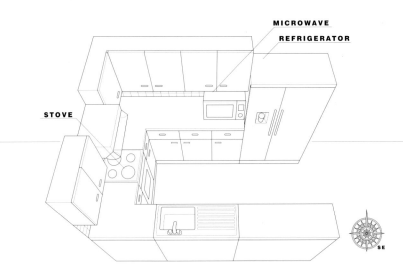

LIGHT MY FIRE
(right)

This plan will need some work to maintain high levels of energy. Paint the cabinets red and place a bowl of floating candles on the countertop.

STARRY NIGHTS
(above)

These floating candles can be placed on the table at informal mealtimes.

TAILOR-MADE
(right)

Kitchen designs are much more flexible these days, and you can choose to have built-in cabinets or freestanding units like this stove in a separate island.

complete your tasks. Adequate storage is essential so that the countertops are clear to use, and there are many space-saving solutions on the market that will help you make the most of a small space.

Good lighting is essential when you are cooking and will make the whole process safer and more enjoyable. The most important lighting will be over the stove, work surface, and sink.

FIERY COLORS

The kitchen belongs to the fire element, or *agni*. A kitchen with a fireplace is ideal and will bring warmth into relationships between the family and with guests. If you do not have a fireplace in your kitchen, and it is not situated in the southeast corner of your home, do not despair. You can boost the fire element by painting your kitchen red, orange, or terra-cotta, the perfect colors for a kitchen. You could repaint the walls, or retile the floor with terra-cotta tiles, but if this does not fit in with your overall scheme, you could just include red or orange splashes of color (such as red flowers or pictures, orange crockery and pans, terra-cotta plant pots—even a red refrigerator). Other fire "boosters" are candles and sun symbols.

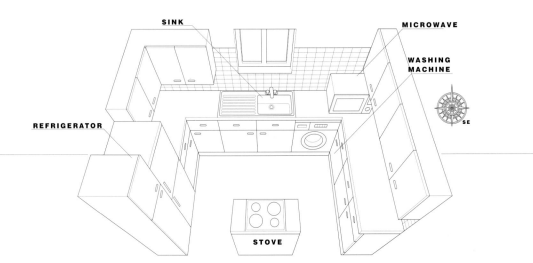

VASTU CHECKLIST — SOUTHEAST

The main gate of a southeast-facing house should be in the east and not in the south. The east is ruled by Indra, king of the gods, and a main gate on the eastern side will bring wealth, happiness, security, and children. A main gate in the southern portion of the home can bring unnecessary anxiety and also a loss of wealth because the south is ruled by Yama, god of dharma and death.

Never keep money or other valuables in the southeast portion of the house, as they may waste away. Keep them in the southwest corner of the northern room of the house.

Telephones should be kept in the southeast corner of the room, especially in the bedroom.

The southeast zone of the house is ideal for reading, research, and creative activities of all kinds. Avoid facing southeast while sitting at your desk, however, as this promotes drowsiness. Radiators, furnaces, stoves, and other electrical appliances should be located where possible in the southeast sector of a room.

The atom is the smallest unit both of the Vedic measurement system and of the universe. The sages believed that measurement of space is related to both the human and the divine world.

If you want a grill in the garden, place it in the southeast corner, as this is governed by fire.

PAINT POWER (*above*)
Dusty pink with stenciled gold decoration is a stylish solution for a southeast-facing kitchen.

FLOWER POWER (*left*)
If you are happy with your décor and don't wish to paint it in fiery red or orange, placing a vase of fire-colored flowers in the kitchen will boost the fire element.

south *direction*

A PERFECT PLAN FOR THE SOUTH (*right*)

The south is the most romantic direction for a bedroom, conducive to nights of passion.

TOP-NOTCH TOPIARY (*above*)

Step up the romance with this unusual heart-shaped plant.

The south is the realm of Yama, the god of death, who is revered by Hindus because all ancestors are in his care. The body, which is believed to consist of the five elements or *panchbhutas*, is left behind on earth and the soul is escorted to the realm of the gods by Yama.

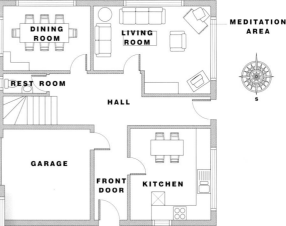

Lord Yama, the embodiment of dharma, is also called the *Dharmaraja* (the king of justice). According to Hindu mythology, Yama is the son of Visvaswat (the sun god, also called Surya). Yama is depicted as green in color, with fiery, red eyes. He wears a red cloak, rides a buffalo, and is armed with a club.

Hindus believe that Yama weighs a person's good and bad deeds on a scale. The soul is sent to heaven, hell, or back to earth to reenter the cycle of birth and death. Good deeds may liberate the soul from this cycle, enabling it to attain eternal happiness by becoming one with God. The

RAINBOW EFFECT (*left*)

Embroidered Indian textiles with mirrored decoration will make any bed look more inviting.

NO MORE BAD NIGHTS *(below)*

For the best night's sleep, your head should face south; east or west are also acceptable. Never sleep with your head facing north. Move the bed so that the head faces south.

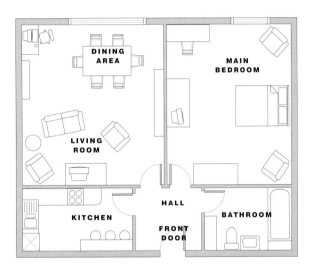

prospect of Yama's judgment inspires people to shun wrongdoing and embrace truth. In this way, Yama eradicates evil and generates qualities such as kindness, justice, truthfulness, honesty, charity, and brotherly love. The other gods associated with the south are Gandharva, Bhrungraj, and Mriga.

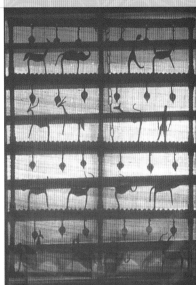

FLOATING SARI *(above)*

Fabulous Indian textiles in reds and pinks will make any bedroom look more inviting.

ALL THE TRIMMINGS *(left)*

This sensual boudoir will bring out the temptress within.

FEMININE CHARMS
(right)

Choose a comfortable bed, fresh flowers, and crisp bed linens for a refreshing night's sleep.

COURTING COUPLE
(below)

Ensure that all images and sculptures in this bedroom are conducive to romance.

THE PLANET MARS

Kuja (Mars) is the planet of the south. He is the god of war, born from the sweat of Shiva and raised by Mother Earth. Kuja is red in color, fiery, and bitter in temperament. He is depicted as a young, handsome, very masculine soldier, with a *tamasic* (dark, passive, lazy), impulsive, and bad-tempered nature. The qualities attributed to Kuja are bravery, strength, patience, energy, and activity. Together with the sun, Kuja heralds the summer, or *Grishma Ritu*. Kuja or Mars is associated with coral (*moonga*) and the color red.

Kuja governs bone marrow, bile, eyes, limbs, and the urinary system, and can cause high fever and problems associated

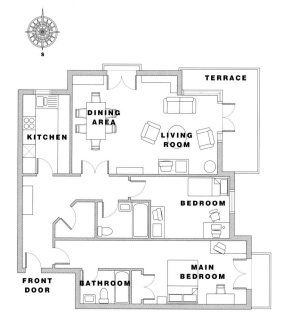

SOUTHERN COMFORT *(above)*

Romance is heightened when the main bedroom faces south. Keep the bathroom door closed to stop the flow of negative energy into the bedroom.

IN THE PINK *(below)*

It may be difficult to move the bed so that the occupants' heads face south; it depends whether the cabinets in the southwest and the dressing table in the south are built in. Otherwise boost the positive energy in the room by decorating it in romantic pinks, and add heart-shaped symbols.

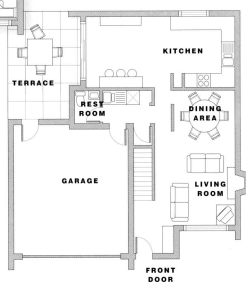

period is associated with the bedroom. Between three and six in the afternoon, the sun heats the south until it glows like embers. From six onward, the south is tranquil again.

ETERNAL FLAME *(above)*

The simple addition of floating candles and essential oils can make a big difference to the atmosphere in a bedroom.

with blood loss and deterioration of the bone marrow. Kuja governs a wide range of activities, including surgery, mechanics, games, sports, the army, property, mining, and minerals. Surprisingly, Kuja is also associated with feminine items such as clothing, jewelry, and cosmetics.

VEDIC TIMINGS

In India, the south receives little sun between three and nine in the morning, so it remains tranquil. Between nine and twelve, there is a smoky light in the south. After twelve, the sun is near the south and at this time, it is *dipta* (lit). This is the time to take a siesta, which means that this

CLASSIC ATTRACTION *(right)*

To make this cool, calm room into a zone of sensuality, close the drapes, turn down the lighting, and light the fire.

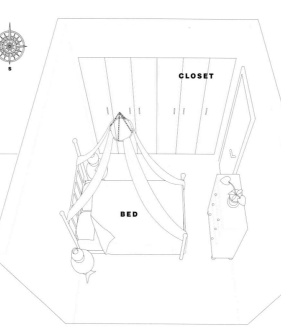

LOVE TRIANGLE

(right)

The bed drapes make a pyramid over the sleepers, which is highly auspicious. For maximum effect, move the bed so that the head faces south.

WARM WELCOME

(below)

Indian images will bring a wealth of color and decoration to your walls.

DEEP SLEEP AND HAPPY DREAMS

Vastu emphasizes the importance of creating an ambience in the bedroom that will bring a feeling of security. This, in turn, encourages the deep sleep that is essential to refresh the mind, body, and spirit.

The south is a good direction for an adult bedroom, as it encourages deep slumber. It is particularly appropriate for romance because the energies of *tamas* (darkness or night) lie here and it is the *guna* (quality) of sleep that inspires physical pleasure, as well as relaxation.

The bed is usually the heaviest item in a bedroom. It should be placed along the southern wall, but about four inches (10cm) away so that the negative energies of the wall do not come in contact with the bed. You should sleep with your head toward the south with your body aligned with the axis of the earth. The *rishis* or ancient sages

believed that this position brought happiness, peace, and *dirghayush* (a long life). If your head is toward the north when you sleep, the north and south poles repel each other, affecting your circulation, disrupting your sleep, and sometimes leading to more long-term health problems. Sleeping with your head to the east or west is preferable to the north, but not as beneficial as facing the south. Make sure your feet do not face south, as this is a bad omen, being the direction ruled by death.

The pictures on the bedroom walls should depict peaceful scenes, rather than ferocious animals or battle scenes. Also avoid pictures of ancestors and family members who have died, as their loss may subconsciously disturb your sleep. Your favorite decorative item or an inspiring picture should be the first thing you see when you wake up in the morning. Make sure your feet do not point toward a sacred picture or object, as this is considered to be offensive.

FRESH FRAGRANCE *(right)*

The scent of fresh flowers in a bedroom will help to create a romantic atmosphere.

COZY COVERS
(left)

Adjustable blinds will keep the moonlight out, ensuring an undisturbed night. The pink check bedspread is the perfect color for a south-facing bedroom.

A bathroom that is connected to the bedroom is not recommended in Vastu. However, if you already have this set-up, make sure the bathroom is to the south or west of the bedroom. Keep the door shut at all times to keep out any negative energies from the toilet.

A FINE ROMANCE

The fragrance of cut flowers, fresh sheets, and bed linens in warm colors are conducive to romance. Enhance the atmosphere in your bedroom even further by placing low lights and fragrant candles around the room. Switch off any central lighting and use special lightbulbs in table lamps to keep the mood mellow.

Stimulate your sense of smell by creating a sensual and soothing atmosphere. Burn jasmine, sandalwood, and rose aromatherapy oil for a romantic setting.

To maintain a warm, loving, and sensual atmosphere, remember to

CHANGING PLACES
(left)

Unless the bed is moved so that the head faces south, its occupants will feel restless and wake tired every morning. Add a soothing or romantic image to the north wall, so that it's the first thing that will be seen on waking in the morning.

CLOSET

ARM CHAIR

BED

S

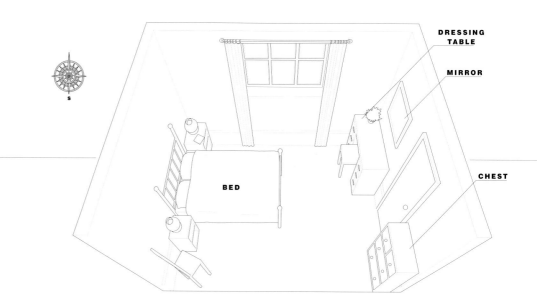

DRESSING TABLE

MIRROR

CHEST

BED

SOFTEN THE LOOK
(right)

It won't take much to move the furniture so that the head of the bed faces south. Then just add soft cushions to the bed and romantic lighting.

QUIET CORNER
(below right)

It's a good idea to have comfortable seating in the bedroom. You may wish to get away from everyone and curl up with a book.

AROMATIC AIR
(below)

The smell of essential oils and incense can either soothe or stimulate the senses.

stimulate all five senses, not just sight and smell. Used with a base oil, rose, jasmine, and sandalwood essential oils can make all the difference to a massage. Enjoy a light meal beforehand—don't overindulge! And because music is said to be the food of love, ensure that you have something melodic playing in the background.

THE COLOR OF LOVE

Shades of red, pink, peach, and terra-cotta are perfect for a romantic room in the south. You could just paint the walls one

color, or use a paint effect such as rag rolling or colorwashing (see pages 62–65) to give the walls a softer, more textural feel. Printed and textured wallpaper designs are available in all styles and you are bound to find one to suit your taste.

Or you could line your walls with fabric; line the fabric with wadding for extra heat and sound insulation. Do be aware, though, that the bedroom is not the place to experiment with clashing patterns or garish hues (no matter how fashionable!). Aim for a serene yet sensual look.

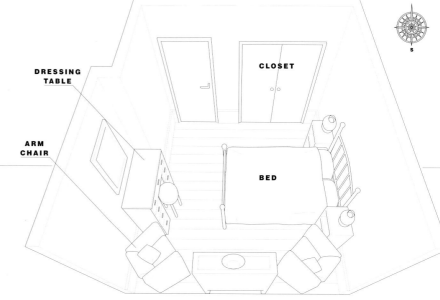

DRESSING TABLE

CLOSET

ARM CHAIR

BED

VASTU CHECKLIST — SOUTH

Whether you are working or relaxing, try to sit with your back to the south to receive the strength and wisdom of your ancestors.

Your home should be higher in the south to encourage good health, wealth, and prosperity.

If the southern portion of the house is lower than the rest of the property, it can lead to ill health and financial problems.

The south is not a propitious direction for an extension because it may lead to financial loss, accidents, and ill health.

The south is a good direction for adult bedrooms. Bedrooms in the south and southwest are especially good for romance. Their connection with the earth element will disturb any studies, so this location is not good for children's rooms.

Leave more open space in the north and east than in the south and west. If possible this space should be more than one and a half times that left in the south and west.

SWEET DREAMS
(left)
Matching the walls and drapes brings tranquility to an opulent bedroom scheme that could otherwise look too busy. The sloping ceiling adds an element of intimacy to the room.

southwest *direction*

A PERFECT PLAN FOR THE SOUTHWEST *(right)*

The southwest is ideal for a main bedroom, as this earth-dominated direction is most conducive to rest and sleep

UNDISTURBED SLEEP *(below)*

Shutters and heavy drapes will keep out any excess light and noise.

The southwest is associated with the earth element, *prithvi*, and with the planets Rahu and Ketu. These are known as *chhaya grahas* (shadow planets) and are important points in the zodiac system.

Rahu and Ketu are the ascending and descending nodes, the points where the path of the moon crosses the ecliptic or path of the sun. The northern point is exactly 180° from the southern point.

Rahu and Ketu are also known respectively as the Dragon's Head

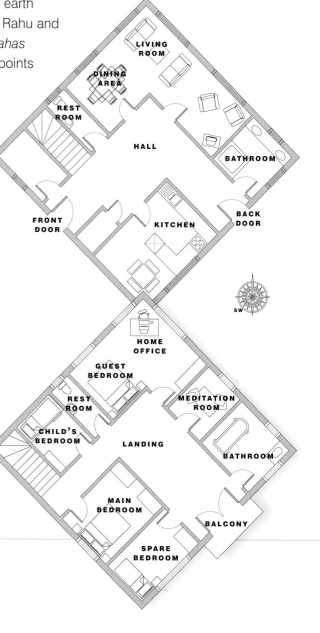

FIT FOR A KING

(right)

This fabulous carved bed is made even more regal by the draped coronet at its head.

nd the Dragon's Tail. Rahu is depicted as tall, dirty, and blue in color. Ketu is depicted as tall and dark gray in color. The gemstone associated with Rahu is *gomed* (cinnamon stone). Ketu's gemstone is *sutramania vaidurya* (cat's eye). Rahu and Ketu are *tamasic* (dark) in nature and symbolize ignorance.

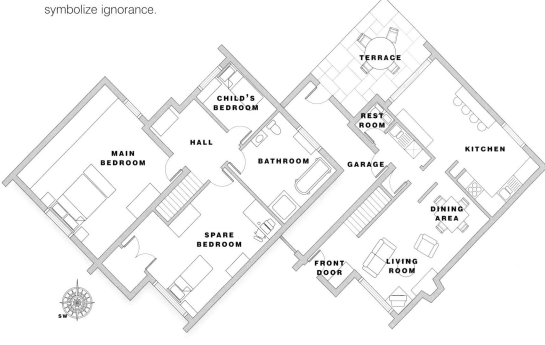

CUSHIONS *(above)*

Use earth-inspired colors such as cinnamon and terra-cotta to add warmth to your scheme.

RESTFUL BEDROOMS *(above)*

The main bedroom is perfectly situated in the southwest, with the bed facing southwest as well. The spare bedroom has been converted into a home office, and the desk faces northeast, which is auspicious.

SLEEPY HEADS *(below left)*

The main bedroom is ideally situated facing the southwest, with the bed facing away from the northeast. The fire element will need boosting with candles in the kitchen and the center of the home should be kept as free from clutter as possible.

VEDIC TIMINGS

In India, between three and six in the afternoon, the rays of the sun reach the southwest of the house. It is a good time for children and students to concentrate on their studies.

THE SOUTHWEST AND YOUR PROPERTY

According to Hindu mythology, the southwest is the abode of the ancestors and *Pittri Kona* is where the south and west

SUN SEEKER
(below)

The plaster walls, marble floors, and earth colors create a stunning effect in this contemporary Indian master bedroom.

KITCHEN

DINING AREA

HALL

FRONT DOOR

BATH ROOM

LIVING ROOM

TERRACE

BEDROOM

MAIN BEDROOM

BALCONY

SW

MAKE IT STABLE (below)

The earth element in the main bedroom needs boosting to increase stability (the northwest is traditionally associated with restlessness, and is more appropriate for a guest bedroom). Paint the room in cinnamon or terra-cotta, and decorate with earth-related images.

meet. Hindus offer *pindas* (balls of rice flour and water) to the *pittris* (forefathers) on the anniversaries of their death as a mark of respect. The southwest corresponds to the feet of Vastu Purusha, so a house with a missing southwest corner is like a person without feet. A missing southwest corner may cause unhappiness.

The southwest section of the home should be higher than all the other directions, because if you respect the *pittris* they will bless your home. If the southwest corner is lower than the rest of your home, this can result in poverty and fear of theft. Tall trees will symbolically raise the height of the property.

When building on a plot you should treat the southwest with caution. If any digging or excavation is required, do not begin with the southwest corner or wall because Lord Yama, the god of death, gains entry to the home from this direction. Underground constructions such

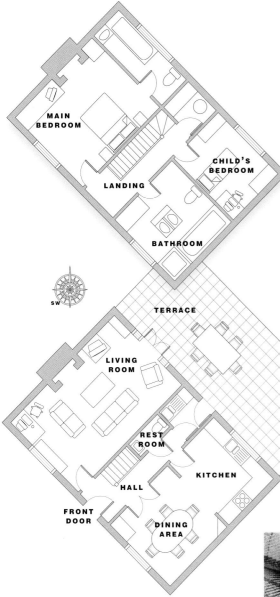

MAIN BEDROOM

CHILD'S BEDROOM

LANDING

BATHROOM

SW

TERRACE

LIVING ROOM

REST ROOM

KITCHEN

HALL

FRONT DOOR

DINING AREA

WALL SCREEN
(above)

Images of fruits, flowers, and foliage are very appropriate for southwest-facing bedrooms.

WARMING WOOLENS
(right)

Earth-colored blankets and throws will keep you warm at night.

BACK TO EARTH
(right)

This romantic four-poster bed has earth-colored cushions scattered across it, to boost the earth element in the room.

as a basement should not be in the southwest. Unobstructed, open space to the southwest of your home may cause family feuds, tensions, incompatibility, and misunderstandings. Do not add adjoining property, a verandah, a balcony, or a deck in the southwest area. However, you may build an annex or outbuildings in the southwest. If the southwest corner of the plot extends in the south, it can result in quarrels within the family and be a cause for constant worry. Such an extension should be corrected by planting trees and bushes. It is inauspicious for a house to be at the end of a road, particularly if it ends in the southwest corner of the property.

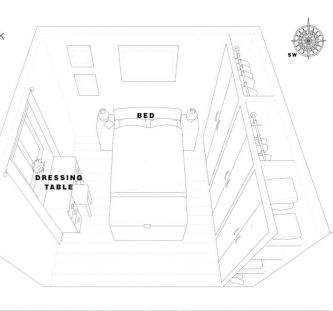

CARVED PANEL *(left)*

Indian decorative carving is renowned for its beauty and intricacy. Position a screen opposite the bed, so that it's the first thing you see on waking up. Don't hang it above the bed; any subconscious uncertainty over its stability will disrupt your sleep.

COMBAT RESTLESSNESS *(above)*

A north-facing bed will bring the occupants restless nights. As the closet is built-in, it will be impossible to move the bed so that the head faces south, but paint the walls with earth colors to boost the earth element and add clay, stone, or wooden carvings.

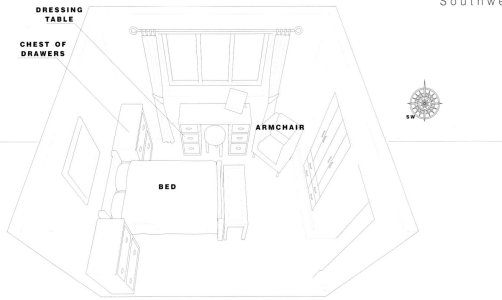

DRESSING
TABLE

CHEST OF
DRAWERS

ARMCHAIR

BED

SW

TO SLEEP, PERCHANCE TO DREAM

The earth element that rules the southwest is conducive to sleep, and the southwest corner is the ideal choice for the main bedroom. The southwest is *tamasic* (*tamasic* attributes are darkness, laziness, passiveness, lack of enthusiasm, and stagnation), and therefore encourages rest.

The bed should be placed along the south wall. Its sheets and covers should always be fresh and inviting. After dark the lights should be dimmed. The dressing table should be along the northern or eastern wall. There should be no religious pictures on the south wall. Children should never be allowed to sleep in a room that faces southwest because the earth element will make them inactive and less likely to study.

EARTHLY DESIRES

Decorate the room in warm, earth colors, such as terra-cotta, rusts, or browns, to enhance the earth element that rules the southwest. Suitable pictures are trees laden with fruits or flowers, and a clay or terra-cotta statue or figurine would be an appropriate accessory. Images of earth in an elliptical orbit, snow-clad mountains, the goddess Parvati, consort of Lord Shiva, and Kamdhenu also

SOFT UNDERFOOT *(left)*
The rich colors of this Indian rug would look stunning against a sisal or wool carpet or wooden floorboards.

MOVE SOUTH *(left)*
Although not ideal, a west-facing bed is acceptable. If you can, move some heavier objects further south; place the armchair against the south wall.

TERRA-COTTA FIGURINE *(above)*
Decorating the room with earth-based sculptures and images will enhance the earth element and help you sleep.

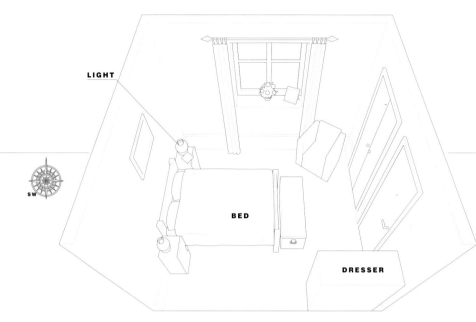

LIGHT

BED

DRESSER

OPTICAL ILLUSION
(above)
These unusual glass vases look like they are made of stone.

A SLIGHT SHIFT
(top right)
The dresser should be moved further toward the southwest to allow easy access around the room. Allow enough space to open the doors with ease.

IN STORAGE *(right)*
Avoid having more than two chests of drawers in your bedroom. Streamline your wardrobe according to the seasons and store those clothes that you don't immediately need.

symbolize the earth element.

The bedspread, upholstery, and bed linen need to be in warm, earthy colors, and the bed and mattress solid and comfortable to ensure a good night's sleep. Close the drapes and keep the light out, lest your rest be disturbed.

CLEVER STORAGE

The southwest is ruled by the earth element, and it is therefore most auspicious to store your heavier items in the southwest of the house and, within each room, in the southwest corner. This

may require some careful planning, to ensure that the storage area is attractive.

In the bedroom, use a hollow window seat for storage, as well as a place to relax. Fitted bedroom closets can be a great way to make a room less cluttered. Buy a bed with drawers that slide into the base, or use storage boxes or wicker baskets under the bed, for storing bed linen, sweaters, or shoes. In the kitchen, choose kitchen units that include drawers, corner carousel shelves, and pull-out trays. Make the space under the stairs into a closet or downstairs toilet.

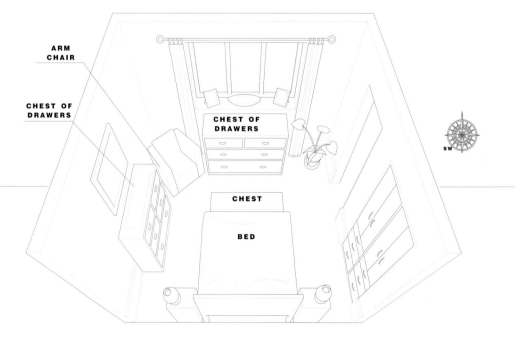

ARM CHAIR

CHEST OF DRAWERS

CHEST OF DRAWERS

CHEST

BED

VASTU CHECKLIST — SOUTHWEST

Heavy items such as *almirahs* (cupboards) and wardrobes should be placed along the southwest corner or wall of the room.

You can construct stairs in the southwest sector of the home. If the staircase is inside, it should not directly face the main entrance. Use the space under the stairs as storage space.

The overhead water tank can be safely placed in the southwest. Make sure it is away from the wall, so that the negative energies of the wall do not contaminate the water.

Temporary structures or sheds can be built in the southwest to reduce open space.

The entrance to the house should not be in the southwest, as it is considered inauspicious.

Women who wish to marry should not sleep in the southwest because it may delay their marriage.

ART AND SOUL
(below)
This unusual main bedroom features a fabulous enclosed bed that is guaranteed to make you feel safe and secure. The decorative bed, ceiling, and paintings are enhanced by the plain walls and wooden floor.

A PERFECT PLAN FOR THE WEST (*below*)

The west is the best direction for a children's bedroom. Ensure that the bed faces south and your child should have a good night's sleep. The west (and southwest) are good for stairs as well.

west *direction*

One of the oldest Vedic deities, Lord Varuna, is the presiding god of the west. Varuna is the god of seas, rivers, and darkness. He is the personification of the sky, the creator of heaven and earth, and ruler of the night. He is depicted riding a *makara* (crocodile). Varuna taught the mysteries of the universe to his son, the sage Vashishtha, an eminent Vastu expert of ancient times. The west is associated with *Shishir* or the winter season.

INDIAN ELEPHANT (*above*)

This charming Indian sculpture will brighten the darkest of corners.

The west is linked to the planet Shani (Saturn). Saturn drives away the beneficial, divine rays of the sun, which make people pleasure-loving, interested only in material comforts and possessions rather than spiritual values.

As the ruler of death, disease, old

CROCODILE SEAT (*right*)

The god of the west, Lord Varuna, is usually depicted seated on a crocodile.

COLOR FIXING *(below)*

Overcome any negative energy in a south-facing child's room by painting the walls light yellow, blue, or mauve (but definitely not the reds and pinks associated with this direction).

age, the skeleton, and the skin, Saturn affects the length of an individual's life. His influence can lead to bouts of depression, loss of strength, and loss of feeling. *Tamasic* (dark, dull, passive) by temperament and representing grief, Saturn is a eunuch or of neutral gender, who symbolizes advancing years, as well as the span of life. The color associated with Saturn is black, but he is also related to blue and to the gemstone *neelam* (sapphire).

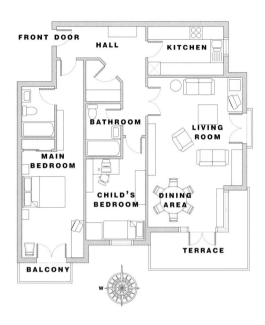

BEAR NECESSITY *(above)*

Keep favorite objects like this bear in your child's room, where it will add to their feeling of security.

BRING ON THE CLOWNS *(left)*

Bright circus-colored storage boxes, shelves, and drawers are ideal for storing toys and books.

STRAIGHT TO BED
(right)

This fun tepee-style bed will entice any young child to bed when the time comes. Triangular drapes are an auspicious shape in Vastu.

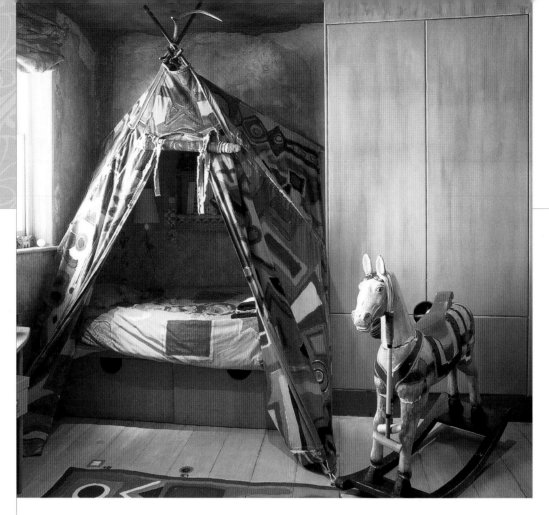

VEDIC TIMINGS

In India, sunset is between six and nine in the evening. This period is known as *Vidya Sala* and the sun is in the west of the house. It is a time for the family to gather for a meal and conversation, or to separate for reading and studying.

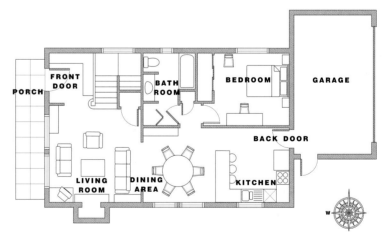

BRIGHT AS A BUTTON *(left)*

Your child's room is used for study as well as play, so set aside a quiet area for this purpose.

WINDING DOWN *(above)*

The best direction for a porch or portico is in the west, where you can sit on a comfortable chair or bench and watch the evening roll in.

AIR TIME *(below)*

This child's room is in the northwest, which could bring a feeling of restlessness. The northwest is ruled by air, so remove air symbols such as fans, wind chimes, model airplanes or hanging mobiles. Also, the bed should be moved to the south wall.

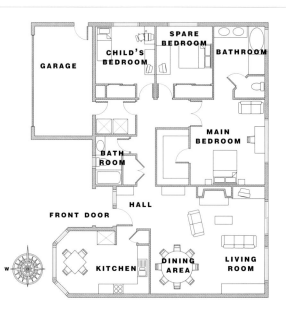

into a room or build a larger balcony on the eastern side. A basement in the west side stores negative energy. A basement in the northwest or southwest is equally bad and should be avoided or filled with stored goods.

However, the west is a suitable location for a portico or porch, although it should not protrude out too much from the main building. Avoid a portico or porch in the

LUCKY SYMBOL *(above)*

Keep a horseshoe in the western area of your home as a good luck symbol.

THE WEST AND YOUR PROPERTY

A west-facing house promotes peace and harmony in all spheres of life, particularly among the family. However, the west should be treated with caution in other respects. A plot with a cut-off portion in the west is undesirable because this will affect the seat and one of the arms of Vastu Purusha.

It is also inauspicious to extend to the western part of the home. Any extension should be separated from the house by a wall or some empty space. A balcony in the west of the building is not beneficial. To remedy a west-facing balcony, convert it

WEST-FACING PORCH *(right)*

Take the time, if you can, to enjoy the last of the evening sunlight.

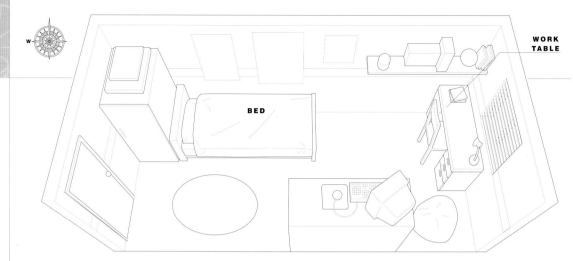

WORK
TABLE

BED

BAD DREAMS

(right)

A child might sleep badly in this room, subconsciously fearing that something might fall from the top of the closet. Moving the bed to the southern wall, with its head facing south, allows for the computer desk to be moved to face north, which is much more conducive to learning. The work table is perfectly positioned facing east.

northwest or southwest because it creates empty spaces on either side. This can be corrected by covering the open spaces at roof level.

If you are constructing a house, you will need to keep in mind a number of things. Any kind of open space in the west should be avoided. If your house faces the west, you can leave more open space in the north, east, and northeast. The boundary wall in the west should be higher than in the east. To raise it, place flowerpots or other items along it. If there is a gate in the west wall, it should be covered with an arch.

WORK AND PLAY

A child's room should be stable yet inspiring, designed for work, sleep, and play. The best location is in the west, placed between the windy northwest and the earthy southwest. The heaviest items, usually the beds, should be placed against the southwest wall or in the southwest corner of the room, slightly away from the wall. If children share a room they should have separate desks, if possible.

SPACE SAVERS *(left)*

Choose a fun bed for your child that will also save on space. Here, the bed is on the top level, while the desk and shelves fit in the space underneath.

The desks should be in the northeast, placed so that the children face the east, northeast, or north while studying (these are all good directions for attaining and retaining knowledge).

Keep the décor light and uncluttered, but do make sure there is enough space for toys and free movement. Light yellow, mauve, and blue are good colors for a child's room. Try to keep the colors on the walls quite subtle, because bright colors may overstimulate young minds. Doors, drapes, storage boxes, and shelves can be more colorful, bringing a sense of fun to the room.

The most important thing is that there be an atmosphere of security, constancy, and—if this is where your children do their homework—mental stimulation. A lamp with a green light on the north wall will

spark the intellect. Avoid putting a television in a child's room, because this will drain their vitality and deprive them of a decent night's sleep.

A BUDDING PICASSO *(left)*

Try to encourage your child's creative streak. Drawing, painting, and writing stories are all ways to tempt them away from the computer or television.

TEEN SPIRIT *(left)*

This excellent layout—with its east-facing work table and chest of drawers in the earth-ruled south—is marred by the bed facing north. Ensure a good night's sleep by turning the bed 45° so that its head faces west.

CHEST OF
DRAWERS

BED

WORK
TABLE

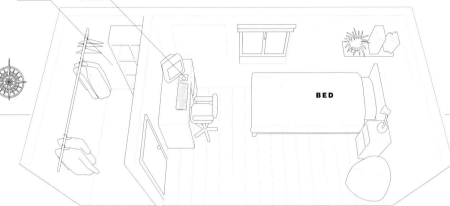

CLOSET

WORK TABLE

BED

ROOMY *(right)*

If you have the room, a walk-in closet is a great way to eliminate clutter. Switch the desk and bed, so that the desk faces east.

A LITTLE TWIST *(bottom right)*

Turn the chest of drawers 45°, so that it sits against the west wall, and bring the bed down to the south wall, with its head facing south. It is this simple to create an auspicious layout.

STAIRS *(below)*

The west and southwest are the most auspicious areas for a staircase.

ONWARD AND UPWARD

The west and southwest are the best areas for a staircase. The ideal staircase is wide, gently curving, and has an odd, not even, number of steps. Steps should proceed from east to west or from north to south. There are a number of options for staircases. Hard floor surfaces are durable and relatively easy to keep clean, but they can be noisy. Polished wood stairs can be slippery, and are especially dangerous in homes where there are children or elderly people.

Carpet is soft underfoot and has sound- and heat-insulating properties, but make sure that it is designed for heavy-duty traffic and is firmly fixed to the stairs. Carpet can also quickly show marks, so avoid very pale colors.

The space under the stairs can be made into a storeroom, and is a great place to house those pieces that aren't in constant use, but that you use enough to need readily available. You could make it into a closet for unseasonal clothes or use it to store sports gear or the children's larger toys. One other option is to convert it into a spare bathroom.

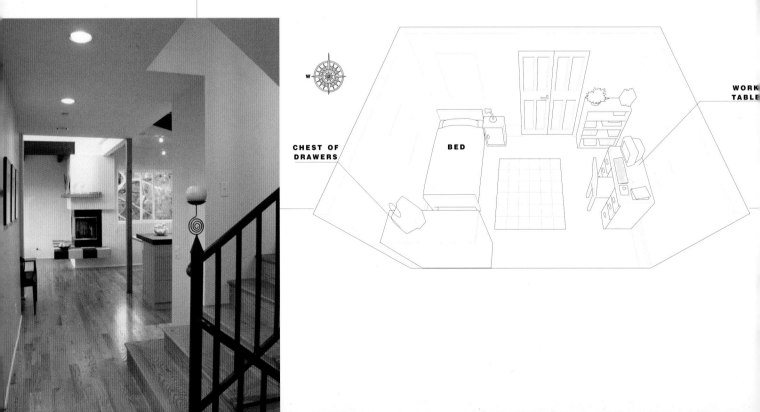

CHEST OF DRAWERS

BED

WORK TABLE

VASTU CHECKLIST — WEST

If a property slopes to the west, it can cause negative energies. If the west is higher than the rest of the property, this promotes prosperity, fame, and a good reputation. Raising the foundation level of the house in the west or lowering it in the east will rectify any problems.

There should be little or no open space in the west so that the energies in your house remain in balance.

The roof of a portico or porch should be higher than that of the rest of the house, as should its floor level. If the portico level or roof is lower than that of the house, the owner may face financial loss and other related problems.

Occupants of a house with a door in the southwest corner of a west-facing house will find it difficult to retain their wealth. Money will flow in and flow out quickly. The door should therefore be kept shut.

TIME OUT *(above)*
Give yourself some time off to enjoy the last rays of the day.

UP IN THE ATTIC *(left)*
The large drawers under the bed, and the chest in the window recess, are perfect places to store toys. This leaves the room clear of distractions for homework at the desk.

northwest *direction*

The meeting point of the north and west is called the *Vayavya Kona*. The presiding deity of the northwest is Vayu, god of wind, and the element that rules the northwest is wind or air (*vayu*).

This direction is also associated with Chandra (the moon). According to Hindu mythology, the moon is the cosmic mother, who influences the reproduction and growth of animals, birds, and plants.

   The moon has an agitated and restless temperament and is associated with movement and the dispersal of goods or wealth. The moon may provoke useless or frivolous journeys, but it also symbolizes riches and peace of mind. Traditionally these riches were agricultural products such as grains or cattle, especially cows. The white or creamy-white pearl (*moti*) is the gemstone of the moon. The feminine moon has a particular influence on women's health, as well as on more general aspects such as nerves, arteries, brain, bladder, stomach, sex organs, and body fluids. If the moon emits

QUEEN OF THE SEA
(*above*)
The pearl symbolizes the moon or Chandra.

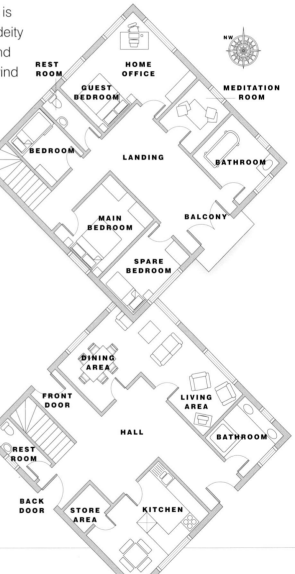

A PERFECT PLAN FOR THE NORTHWEST (*above*)
The dining area is located in the northwest and the restroom and guest bed on the top floor also face northwest. Put up decorative screens for privacy, and to square up the rooms.

THE COSMIC MOTHER *(left)*

The moon (Chandra) presides over the northwest direction.

VEDIC TIMINGS

In India, the northwest is tranquil for most of the day. Between six and nine in the evening, the northwest becomes dusky, or slightly lit. Between nine and midnight, the light of the sun sinks away. In earlier times, this was when all the housework was done, the livestock was cared for, and the family headed for bed. The northwest was the traditional direction for cowsheds and stables; it is now recommended for guest bedrooms.

negative vibes, these can cause insanity or mental instability, and ailments such as jaundice, dysentery, asthma, dyspepsia, bronchitis, gynecological problems, venereal diseases, and fluid retention.

AIR PLAY *(left)*

Use blue plates and napkins in the dining area and blue accessories in the bathroom to boost the wind element.

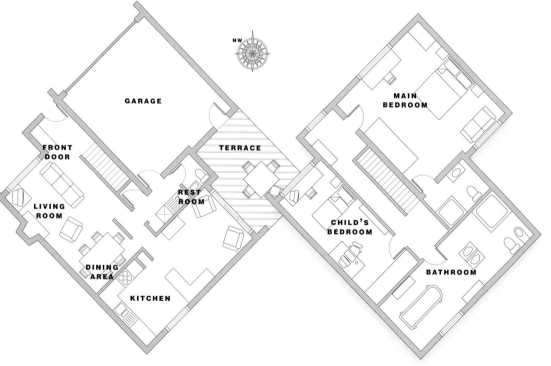

CREATURE COMFORTS *(right)*

Aromatherapy bath oils soothe away the cares of the world. These attractive blue bottles are appropriate accessories for a northwest-facing bathroom.

A REFRESHING BREEZE *(below)*

The dining room and bathroom, situated in the west, will need just a small boost of the wind or air element. Use a wind chime by the window to catch the breeze.

THE NORTHWEST AND YOUR PROPERTY

If your property is missing its northwest corner, this is inauspicious. The missing corner may encourage enemies to your home, and cause theft and burglary. If the house has a northwest extension, family members will travel a lot. A well, a sunken garden, or any other depression in the northwest can bring unhappiness into the home. However, the northwest is an excellent position for a garden, and for covered garages and parking areas.

Within the home, the northwest should not be cluttered, and heavy structures or items here may lead to mental illness,

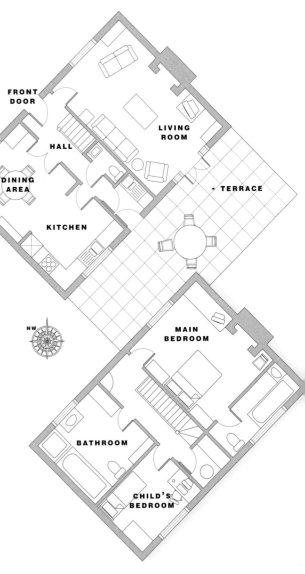

CREATURE COMFORTS *(left)*

The blue walls and airy drapes on the four-poster bed make this guest bedroom very inviting.

TOUCHES OF BLUE *(below)*

The main bathroom, attached to the main bedroom, faces northwest. Keep the door closed so that negative energy does not seep into the rest of the home. Use touches of blue in the west-facing dining area to boost the wind element.

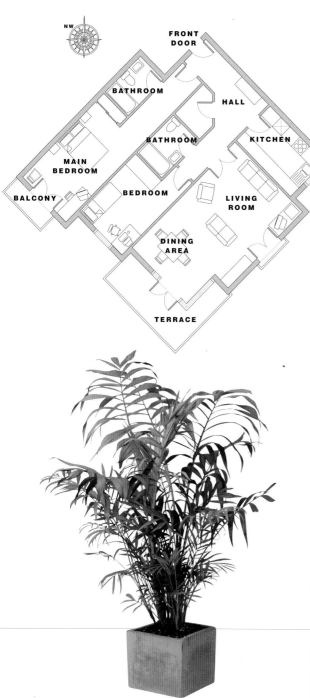

arthritis, osteoporosis and other diseases of the bones, or gastric troubles. The northwest should always be open and spacious. If the kitchen cannot be in the southeast, the northwest is a good alternative, as long as you boost the fire element with fiery colors and fire symbols. Someone recovering from an illness should recuperate in the northwestern part of the house, as the peace and quiet of this direction will aid speedy recovery.

The northwest is the traditional direction for granaries. It was believed that storing

MEDITERRANEAN STYLE *(below)*

Blue or green mosaic tiles are a good alternative to larger tiles or wood paneling, and will withstand the most vigorous bathtime splashes.

LUSH LEAVES *(above)*

Indoor plants look attractive in the bathroom. Choose a type that will enjoy a warm, steamy atmosphere.

CRESCENT MOON *(left)*

The moon symbol is associated with the northwest and will attract positive energy into the home.

EATING IN *(right)*

Ideally, the sideboard should be placed on the south side of the room, where it will "ground" the positive energy, but it is better positioned in the west than in the open east or northeast.

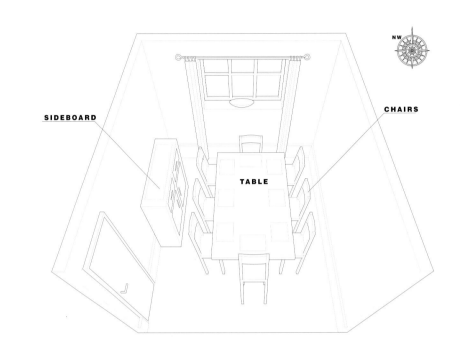

SIDEBOARD

CHAIRS

TABLE

NW

grain in the northwest would ensure that there was never a shortage of food. The northwest is still the best direction for storing provisions.

BLUE MOON

The best color for northwest rooms is a cooling, soothing blue. Whether you tile the bathroom or sponge-paint the guest bedroom, blue is a classic color that will suit a traditional or contemporary scheme.

SQUARED UP *(left)*

A square or rectangular dining table is a more stable shape than a round or oval one. Soften up any hard edges with comfortable cushions.

THE DINING ROOM

Eating food in a group is a bonding experience, whether you are eating with family or friends. It is a chance to catch up with news and to take time out for each other. The northwest is a good area for the dining room, if you have the space for a separate room. The dining area can also be on the western side of the kitchen. If the dining area is in the kitchen, the refrigerator should be placed in the southeast or northwest and the sink in the north or northeast.

The dining table should be square or rectangular, and the chairs occupied by the owners of the house should be placed in the south of southwest and west of southwest. Children or guests can occupy the other chairs.

Avoid using an oval dining table, as its corners are missing (which does not bring stability to the home); a

TABLE

CHAIRS

NW

SIDEBOARD

BRIGHT FLOWERS *(above)*

Fresh flowers always lighten the atmosphere, especially if they have a pleasing fragrance.

WELL PLANNED *(above)*

The heavy sideboard is correctly positioned in the south (the west-facing wall would also be all right). Use candles and low chandeliers to make the lighting more conducive to warm conversation.

UP IN THE ROOF
(right)

This attic bedroom is the perfect space for guests, away from the noise of the rest of the house. The walls are classic yet soothing.

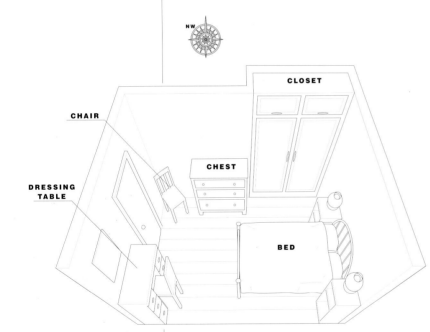

square or rectangle will bring more stability into the home.

At home or at work, try to eat sitting down, away from your desk or the stresses of the day, and concentrate fully on the process of eating. Food eaten during the working day should be light—spicy food and stress are not a good mix. Eat slowly and chew your food well.

Rushing your food will give you indigestion, and if the food is not broken down properly, your body won't be able to get the best nutrients.

MAKING SPACE *(above)*

This guest room is fairly cluttered, which may disturb the guests' sleep. Take out the dressing table and move the bed 45° to the south so that the bed faces south.

A **WARM WELCOME** (*below*)

Guests will sleep well in this south-facing bed. Restore the positive energy lost from the east-facing built-in closets by boosting the air element with a blue-based scheme.

THE GUEST BEDROOM

The guest bedroom should be situated in the northwest, which is ruled by the wind, so that guests are comfortable but don't outstay their welcome. The bed or beds should be placed an inch or so away from the southern or western wall, and guests should sleep with their bodies aligned with the axis of the earth and their heads toward the south (never the north or your guests will have a bad night's sleep). The door of the guest bedroom should not be in direct alignment with the door of the main bedroom, as this could cause unnecessary awkwardness.

Make sure the drapes or shutters shut out most of the light and street noise, and position the beds a little away from the windows and the door to prevent drafts.

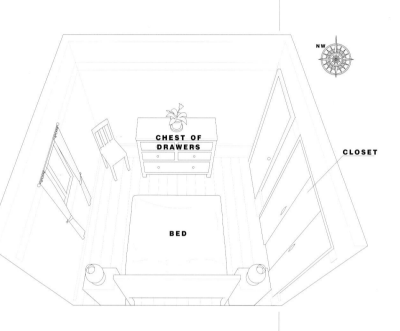

NW

CHEST OF DRAWERS

CLOSET

BED

IN THE LAP OF

LUXURY (*left*)

This self-contained guest room feels like its own little apartment. The splashes of blue boost the air element in this room.

BATHING BEAUTY
(right)

This bathroom is well planned in Vastu terms. All the heavy items are in the south or west, and the door is in the east. With no window in sight, this room will need an exhaust fan.

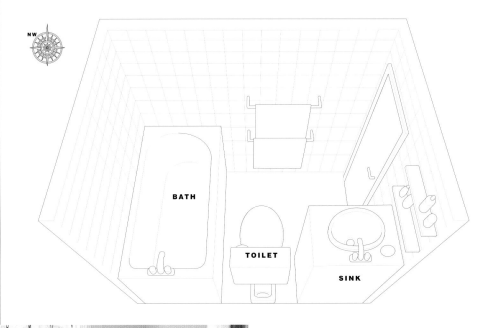

THE BATHROOM

In earlier times in India, people built toilets outside the home to prevent negative energies from entering the house. These rooms were not connected in any way to the main building; they faced away from the home, and were placed in the northwest sector of the property.

Today, inside toilets should still be located in the northwest sector of the home. Bathrooms that are connected to bedrooms should have the toilet on the northwest side of the room. There should be a window to let in fresh air, and the toilet should always be left with the seat and lid

TRADITIONAL SCHEME *(left)*

As Vastu suggests, the toilet is well away from the window and the lid is down to keep out negative energy.

MEDITERRANEAN STYLE *(right)*

A neutral palette and wood paneling makes this a soothing place to bathe.

down. Keep the door shut at all times.

There are certain areas where a bathroom with a toilet should not be positioned, such as the northeast area, as this is a spiritual direction that should be reserved for meditation. The toilet should not be situated right next to the kitchen, because this is unhygienic, and poverty will come to your home if the toilet is just opposite the front door.

Try to keep the toilet away from the window, for privacy, and align the toilet along the north-south line, so that you face north when you are seated.

If your toilet is in any area but in the northwest, you can minimize the negative effects by placing symbols of the element in which it is located. For example, if the

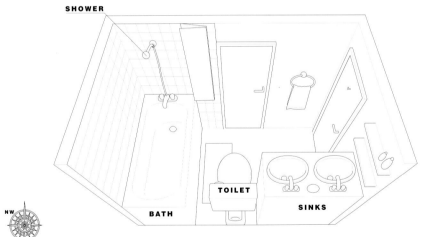

SHOWER

NW

BATH

TOILET

SINKS

MAIN ATTRACTION *(above)*

This bathroom has a door leading to the main bedroom. With the heavy items in the south and west, the plan is in line with Vastu recommendations. However, make sure that the toilet lid is always closed to avoid negative energy.

COUNTRY LIVING
(right)

This rustic dining room with its large vases, objets d'art, and inspiring pictures must surely be a talking point at dinner.

toilet is in the southwest, boost the earth element with plants and earth symbols.

BLOWING IN THE WIND

The wind element may be weak in your home, perhaps because the dining room, bathroom, or guest bedroom are not located in the northwest. In this case, enhance the element by opening more windows in the northwest, letting in fresh air. Install air conditioners in rooms that do not have adequate ventilation. In hot climates, electric fans help keep the atmosphere cool. Boost the wind element further by hanging up wind chimes, mobiles, flags, or decorative objects and jewelry in the shape of a moon. The color blue is associated with the northwest, and it is simple enough to add blue objects or to paint the walls a favorite shade of blue.

VASTU CHECKLIST — NORTHWEST

A bedroom in the northwest is auspicious for young, unmarried girls.

The home should be higher in the northwest than the northeast, but lower than in the southwest and southeast.

The northwest is a favorable direction for romantic encounters. In ancient times, the Ratikaksha—a special room for lovers—was constructed in the northwest sector of the home.

Hang a swing on a tree in the northwest sector of your garden to experience the pleasurable sensation of floating through air.

Decorate the northwest corner of your house with wind chimes and hand fans to boost the wind element.

The best shape for sports arenas and auditoriums is round or oval. The circle is the symbol of Vayu, god of wind, and a circular shape releases energy. It is best to position the sports arena or the auditorium in the northwest sector of a city or town. A circular shape and a northwest position will go a long way toward ensuring a good performance from the players and harmony in the audience.

Keep perishable items such as vegetables and fruit in the northwest portion of the kitchen. This is also a good location for your refrigerator.

LIE BACK AND RELAX *(above)*
This luxurious sunken bath is made more classical with a simple window treatment and paneling.

GLOSSARY

AGNI
The fire element; also the name of the god of fire, who resides in the southeast.

AKAASH
The space element, or ether, the first of the five basic elements created by Lord Brahma.

ANGULA
A Vedic unit of measurement—the length of the middle phalanx of the middle finger of the officiating priest (11/8 inches/3cm).

AYADI
Six formulas for calculating various construction data to ensure that the residents will enjoy good health, good luck, and prosperity.

AYURVEDA
Ancient Indian healing system based on the Vedas.

BRAHMA
The creator of the universe, and the most important of the Hindu trinity, who resides in the northeast.

BRAHMASTHANA
The central space within a building. The *marma sthanas* are located around this area.

DHARMARAJA
The god of justice, also known as Lord Yama.

GANESH
The elephant-headed god of wisdom and fortune.

HASTA
A Vedic unit of measurement—the distance between the elbow and the tip of the middle, first, or little finger.

HAWAN
A sacred ritual performed to Agni, the god of fire, when a baby is born.

INDRA
The lord of heaven and the chief god of the east.

ISA
The god of water, who resides in the northeast.

JAL
The water element.

KUBERA
The god of wealth, who resides in the north.

LAKSHMI
The goddess of wealth.

MAHA BHUTAS
The five natural elements—ether (space), air, fire, water, and earth.

MAHABHARATA
Ancient religious Hindu epic.

MANA
A Vedic unit of measurement—a handspan.

MARMA STHANAS
Points within the Vastu Purusha Mandala that are vulnerable to heavy objects being placed over them.

NIRRITTI
The god of death and destruction, who resides in the southwest.

PARVATI
The mother of the world, the female personification of Lord Shiva, also known as *Kanya*, or Mother Earth.

PRITHVI
The earth element.

PURANAS
Ancient Sanskrit verses, written around the eighth century, about the gods and their families.

RISHIS
The seven authors of the Vedas, who first allotted specific deities to the plan of the mandala.

SARASWATI
The goddess of learning.

SHAKLA PAKSHA
The time between a new moon and a full

moon—considered an auspicious time to move into a property.

SHASTRAS
A set of rules and regulations to follow in daily life.

SHIVA
The god of creation and destruction.

SOMA
The god of liquids, who resides in the northeast.

SURYA
The sun god, who resides in the east.

VARUNA
The god of seas, rivers and darkness, and the presiding god of the west.

VASTU
The ancient Hindu science of design and architecture.

VASTU PURUSHA
Originally a daemon, Vastu Purusha is the Lord of Construction. He is symbolic of the harmful energy that can exist if the spirits of a site are not appeased and the gods blessed.

VASTU PURUSHA MANDALA
A grid representation of the Hindu view of the universe, used by Vastu practitioners as a blueprint for constructing buildings and designing interiors that are spiritually uplifting and harmonious. Each square in the grid is associated with a specific god.

VASTU SHASTRA
The ancient Hindu texts.

VASTUSHASTRI
An experienced Vastu practitioner.

VAYU
The air element; also the name of the god of air, who resides in the northwest.

VEDAS
The oldest Indo-European philosophical documents containing the foundation of Indian thought, culture and sacred law; written in 2500 BCE.

VISHWAKARMA
The architect of the gods.

VISTU VIDYA
A section of the Vastu Shastra that deals specifically with the architectural rules.

YAMA
The god of death, who resides in the south.

BIBLIOGRAPHY

Bansal, Ashwinie Kumar, *Vastu for Lucky Homes* (Fengshui Point Publishing House, New Delhi)

Boner-Sarma-Baumer, *Vastusutra Upanishad: The Essence of Form in Sacred Art* (Noti Lal Banarsi Dass Publishers Pvt. Ltd., Delhi)

Chakrabarti, Vibhuti, *Indian Architectural Theory: Contemporary Uses of Vastu Vidya* (Oxford University Press, Delhi)

Das, Krishna P., *The Secrets of Vastu* (Udaya Lakshmi Publication, Secunderabad)

Gopintha Rao, C.H., *Astrology in House Building* (Gopintha Rao, Madras)

Niranjan Babu, B., *Vastu Relevance to Modern Times* (UBS Publishers Distributors Ltd., New Delhi)

Prabhu, Balagopal T.S. & Achyuthan, A., *Design in Vastu Vidya* (Vastuvidya Pratisthanam, Calicut)

Puri, B.B., *Applied Vastushastra in Modern Architecture* (Vastu Gyan Publication, New Delhi)

Ramachandra, P.N., *An Introduction to Vastushastra* (Bhagyalashmi Stores Book Sellers & Publishers, Bangalore)

Raman, V.V., *Principles & Practice of Vastushastra* (Vidya Bhawan Publisher and Booksellers, Jaipur)

Rao, Muralidhar, *Hidden Treasure of Vastu Shilpashastra and Indian Traditions* (S.B.S. Publishers Distributors, Bangalore)

Sahasrabudhe N.H. & Mahatme, R.D., *Mystic Science of Vastu* (Sterling Publishers Pvt. Ltd., New Delhi)

Sen, Bhanu, *A Dictionary of Vedic Rituals* (Concepts Publishers, Delhi)

Shukla, D.N., *Vastushastra, Hindu Science of Architecture*, two volumes (Munshiran Manoharlal Publishers, New Delhi)

FURTHER READING

Ananth, Sashikala, *Penguin Guide to Vaastu* (Penguin Books, India)

Arya, Rohit, *Vaastu: The Indian Art of Placement* (Destiny Books)

Cox, Kathleen, *Power of Vastu Living: Welcoming Your Soul into Your Home and Workplace* (Pocket Books)

Cox, Kathleen, *Vastu Living: Creating a Home for the Soul* (Marlowe & Co).

Craze, Richard, *Vaastu* (Carlton Books)

Krishna, Talavane, *The Vaastu Workbook: Using the Subtle Energies of the Indian Art of Placement* (Inner Traditions International Ltd)

Pegrum, Juliet, *The Vastu Vidya Handbook: The Indian Feng Shui: Using Vastu Vidya to Bring Harmony and Prosperity into Your Home or Office* (Three Rivers Press)

INDEX

Page numbers in *italics* refer to captions

CREDITS

Quarto would like to thank and acknowledge
the following for permission to reproduce the
pictures:
Key: b=bottom, t=top, c=center, l=left, r=right

Abode Interiors Photography & Library, 77 t,
    79 b, 121 b, 127 b;
Armitage Shanks, 137;
The Art Archive, 15 t(Musée Guimet Paris/
    Dagli Orti);
Dinodia Photo Library, 28;
La Hacienda, www.lahacienda.co.uk, 100 r;
Margaret Howell, 115 b;
Kährs,4 c, 29 t, 49 t, 101 r;
Marshall Editions, 61 t;
Pictures Colour Library, 32;
Pictor International, 8 l, 36, 41 b, 44, 69 t;
Red Cover, 33 (Christian Sarramon);
Kim Sayer©Homes & Gardens/IPC Syndication,
    97 b;
Nicholas Springman design, 54 c;
Trip, 14 (H.Rogers), 45 r (H.Rogers)
Elizabeth Whiting & Associates, 6, 29b, 37, 41 t,
    45 l, 74 t, 75 b, 81 b, 89, 90, 92, 95, 104 b,
    105 b, 109, 111 b, 113 t, 114, 119 b, 122 t,
    124, 130, 131 b, 132 b, 134 t, 135, 138, 60,
    61 br,
Christopher Wray Lighting, 591-593 King's Rd,
    London SW6 2AP, www.christopherwray.com,
    76 l, 58-59;

Thanks to Jaipur Designs, 13 Goodge St,
London W1T 2PG for allowing us to photograph
their Indian handicrafts